Preparation for Classroom Teaching

Don Barnett
Douglas Smith

HARCOURT
BRACE
CANADA

Harcourt Brace & Company, Canada
Toronto Montreal Orlando Fort Worth San Diego
Philadelphia London Sydney Tokyo

Preparation for Classroom Teaching

Canadian Cataloguing in Publication Data

Barnett, Don C.
   Preparation for classroom teaching

Includes bibliographical references and index.
ISBN 0-7747-3426-4

1. Teaching.   I. Smith, Douglas J. (Douglas James),
1938–   .   II. Title.

LB1025.3.B37 1993   371.1'02   C93-094805X

Preface

This book is designed to develop teachers as reflective decision-makers who are able to discover and critically examine principles of instruction. The contents are related to the changing nature of contemporary society; hence, the attention to issues such as teaching in multicultural contexts, adjusting to varied learning styles, counteracting drug and child abuse, helping the learning-disabled, and working with students who are living in poverty. These issues demand attention in any textbook purporting to reflect the needs of teachers in classrooms today.

Discussions, interviews, and educational conferences with inner-city teachers and teachers of multi-ethnic students and students with special needs have provided a basis for a good deal of the content.

The book draws from several philosophical orientations (behaviourism, humanism, etc.) rather than a single perspective. Teaching is a complex process and no single philosophy or teaching technique is sufficient to meet the needs of students diverse in backgrounds and experiences. Theories and models are applied to actual classroom teaching situations and school subject areas.

Chapters are organized around key objectives and concepts. Specific skills and teaching procedures are outlined within the context of current classroom situations.

Examples to clarify theories, principles, and models are drawn from both the elementary and the secondary level. Although the authors recognize the uniqueness of teaching at the primary, elementary, or secondary level, the work is premised on the belief that there is a great deal of commonality in teaching at all grade levels.

The basics of effective teaching — the school curriculum, asking questions, techniques of classroom management, planning, evaluation procedures — are included here, but the book goes beyond this basic level to address the issues facing the Canadian teaching force today.

Acknowledgements

P. 27 Figure 3.3: Adapted and reprinted with the permission of Macmillan Publishing Company from THE ESSENTIAL MIDDLE SCHOOL, Second Edition, by Jon. W. Wiles and Joseph Bondi Jr. copyright © 1993 by Macmillan Publishing Company.

P. 74–75. Student Activities and Methods, and p. 76 The Day Plan: Reprinted with the permission of Bocam Publishing from TEACHING SOCIAL STUDIES by Don Barnett, copyright © 1987 Saskatoon: Bocam Publishing Company.

P. 117–118 Cooperative Learning: From Johnson, D.W. and R. Johnson (1991). LEARNING TOGETHER AND ALONE: COOPERATIVE, COMPETITIVE AND INDIVDUALISTIC LEARNING, Third Edition, Englewood Cliffs, N.J.: Prentice Hall.

P. 118–119 Jigsaw: From Slavin, R. (1983). COOPERATIVE LEARNING, White Plains, N.Y. Longman.

P 121 Uses of Computers: Reprinted with the permission of Macmillan Publishing Company from INSTRUCTIONAL MEDIA AND THE NEW TECHNOLOGIES OF INSTRUCTION, Third Edition, by Robert Heinich, Michael Molenda and James D. Russell, copyright © 1989 by Macmillan Publishing Company.

P. 126–131 Instruction of Special Subjects and Specialities: Guidelines were prepared by authors after consultation with instructors in Teacher Education, (1992), Saskatoon: University of Saskatchewan.

P. 156, Summary for good rules: From C. Evertson, (1987), Managing Classrooms, In D Berliner & B. Rosenshine (Eds.) TALKS TO TEACHERS 93-110., New York: Random House.

P. 161 Figure 11.7. Adapted from D. Orlich, R. Harder, R. Callahan, D. Kauchak, R. Pendergrass, A. Keogh and H. Gibson, (1990). TEACHING STRATEGIES, Third Edition, D.C. Heath and Co: Toronto.

P. 164–165, The Teacher as Listener: Adapted from Barr Films, (film) LISTENING THE PROBLEM-SOLVER copyright © 1981, Gordon Watt Films.

P. 166–167 Communication Skills: Reprinted with permission from Northwest Regional Educational Lab., Portland, Oregon, TRAINER'S MANUAL: INTER-PERSONAL COMMUNICATIONS by John, L. Wallen, 1968.

Contents

PART III: APPROACHES TO INSTRUCTION

PART IV: CLASSROOM INTERACTIONS

Part I:
BACKGROUND TO TEACHING

Chapter One:
WHAT IS GOOD TEACHING?

MAIN UNDERSTANDINGS

In this chapter you will learn the following:

1. Many variables affect the performance of a teacher.
2. "Good" teaching needs to be defined within its proper context.
3. Different variables become more or less influential, depending on whether the teacher's focus is on academic achievement or on attitude or skill development.

It is difficult to define "good" teaching. The many studies that have attempted to do so have often produced contradictory findings. Do students learn more from a clear and motivating lecture, or is hands-on or group work more effective? Does providing students with an initial overview of course content help them to learn more effectively, or not?

There is no simple answer to the question "Which method of teaching is most effective?" Studies conducted at the University of Canterbury in New Zealand (Wright and Nuthall, 1970) showed that students achieved higher grades when teachers emphasized covering the content. Other teaching activities (giving directions, asking questions, etc.) were less influential.

3

COMMON FACTORS IN GOOD TEACHING

Even though the findings from each research study need to be viewed in their own context, early studies on effective teaching help to pinpoint the common characteristics of good teaching. Rosenshine (1983) identified factors such as enthusiasm, warmth, organizational ability, businesslike orientation, clarity of expression, use of probing questions, and variety of teaching materials. These teachers were seen to make optimal use of class time, and had expectations that students would complete a certain amount of work every period.

Brophy and Evertson (1978) found that good teachers exhibited persistence and had a "can-do" attitude, whereas poor teachers tended to become easily frustrated by similar teaching problems. Better teachers assumed control and took full responsibility for selecting content and method. They incorporated material which related to the personal lives of students. These teachers monitored the whole class and moved around the room to check on students' progress with deskwork.

Good and Grouws (1981) studied effective middle years (Grades 6-8) math instruction and found that daily systematic instruction with review, whole-class instruction, modelling, and group and individualized practice resulted in higher standardized test scores for students who received the instruction compared to those who did not.

Classroom observations during studies conducted in California during the early 1970s (McDonald 1976) identified characteristics of teachers who operated more effective classrooms. These teachers called students by name and got all the students involved in classroom decision-making. They were able to adjust to unexpected events or emergent instructional opportunities, and used these events and opportunities to the advantage of learning. These characteristics contributed to mutual respect between teachers and students.

Being businesslike and verbally fluent is important

McDonald also found that the more effective teachers were able to focus on the *relationships* between ideas or events, rather than merely teaching about one idea or a chain of events.

These studies also noted that the better teachers were verbally fluent, while poorer teachers spoke vaguely. McDonald identified several words or phrases which contributed to vagueness: "somewhere," "all of this," "not very," "almost," "pretty much," "anyway," "of course," "excuse me," "not sure," "sometimes," and "often." In the following example, an English teacher's effectiveness is undermined by vagueness.

This story *might* help us understand *somewhat* more the reasons underlying behaviour in young people your age. *Maybe* before we discuss *probably* the main theme of the story, we *should* review a few new terms. *Actually,* the first term is "fairness." *As you know,* fairness *may* be seen from the perspective of the individual . . . *uh, I mean, uh,* beauty is in the eye of the beholder, *you know what I mean.*

FIGURE 1.1
FACTORS IN GOOD TEACHING

Positive Factors	Questionable Factors
Covering the content	Not covering the content
Focusing on relationships between ideas	Teaching a chain of events or ideas in isolation
Enthusiasm and warmth	Silence
Involving all students	Concentrating on subgroups of students
Verbal fluency	Verbal vagueness
Clarity	
Organization	
Businesslike approach	
Probing questions	
Persistence	
Participation	
Calling students by name	
Using unexpected events to advantage	

TEACHING FOR ACADEMIC ACHIEVEMENT

Factors important in teaching for academic achievement are sometimes different from factors which come into play if you are teaching to improve students' attitudes. For example, Brophy and Evertson (1978) found that the achievement scores of junior high school students increased when teachers spent most of the time focusing on academic activities. These teachers interacted with their students on a teacher-pupil basis, rather than on a friend-to-friend basis. Teachers who spent more time focusing on personal relationships and feelings were less effective in teaching for achievement. The lowest achievement scores were shown by students whose teachers demonstrated a disillusioned or embittered personality in the classroom.

Studies by Jane Stallings *et al.* (1979) with junior high and high school students have shown that the more time spent on instruction, the higher the lever of achievement. There are, of course, variations in the effective use of time.

In the above-mentioned study, Brophy and Evertson (1978) also found that overall achievement was greater when discipline problems were kept to a minimum and when teachers were generous in their praise of students' efforts.

These findings were supported by a study conducted by Good, Grouws and Ebmeier in 1983. Better teachers had better-managed classes even when there were more students in these classes than in those of less successful teachers. The better teachers were able to spend less time on "transition" (moving from point to point during classes and changing focus within the lesson) and in disciplinary activities. Students were encouraged to call out more answers and ask more questions.

The studies also noted that effective teachers were pleasant but businesslike, were more knowledgeable, carefully monitored student progress, and took personal responsibility for the academic progress of their students.

Levels of comprehension increased when the day's lesson was related to a major concept or unit of study. A recognizable lesson structure such as "tell them what you're going to tell them, tell them, then tell them what you told them" appears to facilitate learning. Review, modelling of new material, guided practice, and independent practice is an effective structure as well.

Madike (1980) noted higher grades on the part of students of Grade 9 teachers who included questioning, summary, and conclusions at the end of lessons, and verbal cueing (calling attention to important content).

Ausubel (1960) concluded that teachers in Grades 5-7 Social Studies enhanced student achievement when "organizers" were used. For example, these teachers might say "Today we're going to do the following . . ." or "Turn on your computers and then I'll explain the procedures for doing Logo Math."

Flanders (1970) found that student achievement was greater when teachers were flexible enough to adapt techniques to a specific situation rather than using the same technique all the time.

For example, an elementary teacher might capitalize on the excitement generated by a visit to the local fire hall to teach the placement of vowels in the words "Fire Chief."

TEACHING FOR POSITIVE ATTITUDE DEVELOPMENT

Positive attitude development is often associated with higher academic achievement. Good and Grouws (1981) reported that in learning mathematics, positive student attitude and classroom climate were rated higher even though the emphasis was on content. The Brophy and Evertson (1978) studies with junior high school students found that student attitudes were most positive when students perceived their teachers as "nice." The classroom was described by students as "enjoyable and undemanding." These math students demonstrated a more positive classroom attitude when they were taught in a way that made them feel successful and capable of accomplishing difficult tasks.

> **Knowledge alone does not guarantee a positive attitude**

Studies in Australia found that college students became *more* prejudiced against aborigines when studies of aboriginal culture emphasized content and provided few opportunities to express feelings or attitudes. Merely increasing knowledge of other racial or ethnic groups will not reduce or eliminate prejudicial attitudes unless the lesson also provides opportunities to experience what it feels like to be discriminated against.

FIGURE 1.2
TEACHING FOR ACHIEVEMENT AND TEACHING FOR ATTITUDE

Teaching for Academic Achievement	Teaching for Creativity and Attitude
Teacher-pupil basis of interaction	Concern for personal relationships and feelings
Frequent teacher praise in class	Enjoyable and undemanding classroom discussions
Well-managed class	
Less time spent on transitions — quick pace	Discussion and opportunities to express feelings
More student responses	Group discussions
More questions by teacher	Interpersonal interactions among students
More questions by students	Co-operative projects and themes
Knowledgeable about subject matter	Experience of success in group interaction
Pleasant but businesslike	Often related to higher achievement
Carefully monitored student progress	
Structuring content — breaking content down into small manageable parts, — reviewing and relating each part	
Organizers at beginning and/or near end of lessons	
Flexibility: adjusting and changing techniques	
Closure with questions at the end of lessons	
"Cueing" — verbal attention to important content	
Focus on key concepts	
Summaries and reviews throughout the lesson	

Feelings of prejudice are reduced when both cognitive and affective dimensions are explored in the classroom. Group discussions and interpersonal interactions are more effective than formal lectures in enhancing attitudes. Experiences such as co-operative interracial learning teams, where students share responsibility for the learning of the whole group, can be highly effective. Similarly, sports teams and classroom work groups have been shown to be positive influences, especially when members of the group experience success in these activities.

Numerous studies have addressed the question "Which is more effective in teaching: process or content?" In "process" teaching, the instruction engages students in an activity and arouses their emotions through games, discussions, or role-playing. In "content" teaching, the instructor presents content or has students locate and recall information. Early studies by Flanders (1970) described "indirect teaching," in which teachers did more questioning and less lecturing. These teachers encouraged students to expand on their ideas, offered praise for students' efforts, and accepted appropriate feelings expressed by their students. Other studies, such as those by Rosenshine (1983), indicated that indirect teaching was less effective than a more direct approach. In these studies, effectiveness was measured in terms of academic achievement rather than attitude or creativity. This illustrates the critical point that the teacher's intent must be considered in order to judge the effectiveness of a teaching approach.

Chapter Two:
THE TEACHER'S PERSONALITY

Main Understandings

In this chapter you will learn the following:

1. A teacher's personality, which can be changed to some extent, is a major factor in being an effective teacher.
2. People grow through three stages of professional development.
3. Good teachers have some common personal characteristics.
4. Awareness of authoritarian personality characteristics can help a person become more open-minded.
5. Awareness of one's own personality helps teachers accommodate students with different personalities.

"Good Teacher" Personalities

Good teachers are people who know their subject. They understand their students. They are flexible and offer a variety of activities and ideas during their classes. They are innovative and adaptable.

One can develop a more effective teaching personality

Good teachers put students first. They have a strong sense of justice. They recognize what is fair and will not hesitate to "go to bat" for students. Too often school regulations and schedules are maintained for the convenience of the teaching staff and at the expense of students. The student-focused teacher will work to change practices that are not in the best interest of students.

A high energy level is another characteristic of good teachers. Many of them undertake extracurricular activities.

A sense of humour is also fundamental. Humour will carry you through uncountable rough sections in teaching. Teaching should be fun. Your students are full of life and laughter. By laughing with students, teachers show their sensitivity to students' perspectives, facilitate the development of a positive classroom climate, and defend against teacher stress.

Good teachers believe in what they are doing. This sense of worth spills over to your students. They recognize your commitment and will respond accordingly. Successful teachers have developed a sense of confidence. Although they are not braggarts, they want to share what they believe to be good ideas. These teachers are optimists. They feel that students can learn. They hope that improvement will occur.

Positive teachers end up with positive students

PERSONALITY, PERSPECTIVES AND TEACHING

One's personality can and does change over time and through experience. Therefore it is possible to develop a more effective teaching personality.

One's personality can also be adapted to suit different situations. Teachers may have a "teacher personality" which they use in the classroom but not at home or at a staff party.

With the realization that these two factors can come to bear on personality, it is now possible to inquire into some important perspectives of personality which influence our effectiveness as teachers.

CONTENT VERSUS PROCESS

Look at the following pairs of alternatives and select the one which is more important to you.

1. Learning subject matter, or acquiring critical thinking skills?
2. The class as a whole, or individuals within the class?
3. High academic standards for the whole class, or different standards for individual students?
4. Schedules and deadlines to be set and maintained, or flexible scheduling and deadlines?
5. Strong teacher leadership and guidance, or group dynamics and problem-solving?
6. Teaching the curriculum content, or teaching according to students' interests?
7. School dances and other social activities are of little importance, or are they important?
8. Staying on the topic, or letting the class's interests lead from the topic?

If your choice was most often the first of each pair of alternatives you are probably, at this time, a content-oriented teacher to whom the subject is of primary importance. You believe that students come to school to learn, and that the teacher's job is to help them learn.

If you chose more of the second alternatives you are probably, at this time, a student-centred or process-oriented teacher. Content is less important to you than the student or the process of learning.

It is important to recognize that a person does not have to be strictly one kind of teacher or the other, and that neither type is necessarily better than the other. Many good teachers possess both kinds of characteristics. The most important considerations are: "To what extent am I oriented toward one position or another?" and "Should I change to some degree, or am I satisfied with my teaching style at this time?"

STAGES OF PROFESSIONAL GROWTH

Fuller and Bown (1975) suggest that teachers can develop through three major stages of professional growth.

The first stage is a "me" focus, in which the major concerns are self- and survival-oriented. Interns and beginning teachers frequently are in this stage. Teachers at this stage ask: "Will I teach a good lesson?" "Will the students like me?" "How will my administrator evaluate my teaching?" "Can I get this topic organized?".

```
DEVELOPMENTAL STAGES
   1. "ME"
   2. CONTENT
   3. STUDENTS
```

Through experience, the new teacher acquires the confidence that "me" is all right. You discover that you *can* teach. You *are* able to organize and deliver a lesson. Students *do* respond to your questions. Once this realization occurs, a teacher is able to move on to the second stage of professional development.

In the second stage, teaching the subject assumes primary importance. Teachers become subject/content experts. Unfortunately, at this stage some overzealous teachers attempt to teach massive amounts of content beyond their students' ability to digest it.

Some teachers may move to a third stage in which they focus on the student. These teachers come to realize that what is most important in the educational process is neither themselves nor the subject they teach, but the students. Content becomes a vehicle to develop students' abilities. The students become the centre of attention and provide the rationale for teaching.

There is no guarantee that every teacher will automatically move through these three stages. A teacher with many years of experience can remain in the content-focus stage, whereas a younger teacher can quickly come to focus on the students and their needs.

ASPECTS OF PERSONALITY

In Chapter 3 we will examine the interaction between a teacher's learning style and the various learning styles of students. But first, think about your own personality. You probably have some unique preferences for learning which will have an impact on your students. Which of each pair of alternatives that follows applies to you? Respond to each question quickly and honestly. Your initial reaction is generally indicative of your basic orientation. There are no completely right or wrong responses. The effect of these personality characteristics on students' learning depends upon the context in which they are considered.

1. Are you a talker and a sharer, or a quiet, introverted person?
2. Are you a decision-maker, or a wait-and-see person?
3. Do you like order and harmony? Do argument and conflict upset you, or are these things not important?
4. Is what others think of you or your ideas important, or are you not bothered much by what others think?
5. Do you like to try new ideas, or are you more comfortable with familiar things?
6. Is praise from others important to you, or not?
7. Is justice important to you, or not?

8. Are you sensitive to the feelings of others, or not?
9. Do you like to follow a plan, or are you comfortable with unexpected changes?
10. Do you tend to start things but not always finish them, or do you prefer to finish one job before starting another?
11. Do you like to be "in the know," or do you not care?
12. Are you a person who makes up your mind and acts on it, or do you have a hard time making up your mind?
13. Do you tend to challenge ideas, or do you generally accept them?
14. Do you like to win arguments, or do you tend to accept others' points of view?

Try to draw some generalizations about your personality on the basis of how you responded to the questions. Do you tend to be extroverted? Are you more of a follower than a leader? Are you more task-oriented or people-oriented? Do you tend to be a compromiser, a conciliator, or a challenger?

After you have selected the alternatives that apply to you, consider the following: How could these traits affect your behaviour as a teacher? How would you tend to treat students? What do these things mean for planning and organization? How would you deal with students who have personality characteristics opposite to yours?

> **It is the interplay of numerous personality characteristics of the teacher and students that makes the classroom such a dynamic focus of interaction. This interplay can either enhance or inhibit the optimal environment for learning.**

Personality Clashes Between Teacher and Student

The following example illustrates how a clash of personality types can influence teacher effectiveness.

Sally has never had a better teacher. Her teacher is organized, maintains clear guidelines and deadlines, and instructs in a logical step-by-step manner which, to her, makes all the pieces fit together in a meaningful way. Sally also is an organized, time-efficient person. For her, learning is a matter of sorting out the steps and linking them together in linear fashion.

On the other hand, Sally's classmate, Leanne, can't seem to hit it off with their teacher. Leanne can't stand the way the teacher insists on perfect order and reason. Leanne would rather explore many possibilities and consider tentative answers. To her, the world is not, nor should it be, defined in black and white terms. Deadlines and organized structure act more as barriers to learning the real meaning underlying things than as helpful guideposts in the learning process.

The teacher is an extrovert. Sally, also an extrovert, thinks the teacher is great. Leanne is more introverted. She is more subjective and personal in her view of things; Sally is more objective, looking for the facts. Sally is more decisive; Leanne wonders more how her choices might effect others. Sally and her teacher prefer a high degree of organization and order. Leanne prefers to be more spontaneous and flexible rather than have everything planned in advance.

The example illustrates how students with different personality types can perceive teachers differently. It also illustrates that the classroom contains many types of personalities, and, to be effective, teachers need to accommodate these differences.

When teachers have some awareness of their own basic personality characteristics, they can begin to appreciate similar and different personalities among their students.

Variations in personality can help explain why some teachers are "better" teachers with some students but not with others

---

Authoritarianism

Rokeach (1960) attempted to analyze teachers' personalities in terms of "open-mindedness" and "closed-mindedness." His Dogmatism Scale purported to investigate the open or closed character of an individual's belief system.

Rokeach identified several characteristics of the authoritarian personality. These were an in-group/out-group orientation; a view of the world in terms of dichotomies, characterized by a lack of spontaneity, originality, or sense of humour; a tendency to search for absolute solutions; a tendency to try to control everything within one's environment; a tendency to uncritically accept the attitudes and morals of authority figures; an inability to tolerate ambiguity or closeness with others; and an inability to vary one's response, with the result that one acts in the same manner in all situations.

The open-minded individual may be described as one who accepts the rights of others to their opinions. Open-mindedness means that the individual may reject another's view, but still recognize the right of the other person to maintain that particular view. In contrast, the closed-minded person rejects both the view and the right of another person to hold that view.

Authoritarian personalities tend to gravitate to education because teaching is a situation in which the authoritarian has the opportunity to exercise power over others.

Can you think of any of your former teachers who possessed these characteristics? Do you know any non-teachers who exhibit these tendencies? Where do *you* fit on the scale between open- and closed-mindedness?

It is possible to be open-minded in one situation and closed-minded in another. Someone who is both a teacher and a parent might be willing to experiment with various teaching methodologies and recognize that different approaches can work for different teachers, but might accept no other view in regard to the raising of his or her own children.

Assertiveness

Teachers need to develop a set of interpersonal skills which enable them to stand up for their rights, clarify their values, and become stronger individuals without becoming aggressive or obnoxious. This ability or skill is called assertiveness. By being assertive we can learn to express our feelings while improving our relationships with students. Teachers can also model assertive behaviour for students who need help in getting their own needs met.

Teachers need to demonstrate assertiveness when communicating with their students and their supervisors. You have the right to tell students "I don't know." You have the right to say no without feeling guilty. You have the right to say to your supervisor "I'll make mistakes and be responsible for them." Teachers have to exhibit a degree of assertiveness as class leaders and as colleagues dealing with other professionals.

In contrast, the aggressive teacher who is too authoritarian or too much of a disciplinarian will invite challenges from today's students. At the other extreme, the passive teacher who fails to enforce reasonable demands will be taken advantage of by students. The effective teacher avoids both extremes.

FIGURE 2.1
TEACHER PERSONALITIES

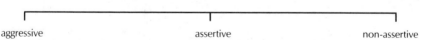

aggressive   assertive   non-assertive

Attitudes Toward Multi-ethnic Students

High mobility within Canadian society, increased immigration, and greater global trading and travel mean that you are likely to teach many students of racial, ethnic, linguistic, and cultural backgrounds different from your own. How will you view these students?

We tend to regard people who are different from ourselves as strange and perhaps even inferior, even though this is illogical. (For instance, students are different from teachers, but this does not automatically make them inferior!)

Assuming that others who are different are inferior is a very destructive personality trait in a teacher

---

The following are some characteristics of a prejudiced attitude, and some ways to counteract them.

1. Prejudiced people tend to look for visible minorities within a group rather than look for individual non-visual characteristics. To counteract this, a teacher should think in terms of individual characteristics and variations of people within a group. Recognize the wide range of differences that exist within any race or class of people, just as these differences exist within your own group.
2. Prejudiced people tend to see differences rather than similarities between or among groups. It is essential that the teacher emphasize the many similarities among groups.
3. Prejudiced people tend to adopt stereotypes. A teacher should encourage students to resist the tendency to reach premature conclusions about others.
4. Prejudiced people tend to identify external attributes rather than internal attributes of individuals. Viewing individuals in terms of external attributes such as hair and eye colour, clothing, and wearing beards should be minimized. More attention should be given to internal attributes of people (Are they warm people? Are they kind?). Use positive labels when considering these internal attributes.

How well will you be able to work with students from different backgrounds?

Effective teachers of multicultural students exhibit the following characteristics:

1. An *interactive posture*. These teachers adapt to the community, taking part in local community affairs, playing games with their students, and visiting people in their homes. They are not aloof or withdrawn,

and they reach out both in the community and within their class-rooms.

2. *Physical closeness.* These teachers work with students at their desks. They sit with them in groups. They are listeners rather than tellers. They wipe kids' tears away and help them blow their noses. Although the physical closeness factor is not so relevant in secondary school or accepted in contemporary society, the "closeness" factor involving empathy and understanding remains extremely important in teaching.

3. *Respect* for the other culture. Different customs are accepted as legitimate behaviour for that cultural group.

4. *Empathy.* These teachers display compassion and affinity for others and can see themselves in the other person's position. Empathetic teachers are able to see the situation from the perspective of the student from the minority culture.

5. *Tolerance for ambiguity.* Ability to suspend judgment is a key ingredient in this quality. People who can tolerate the uncertainties of working with another cultural group become more effective teachers.

6. *High but realistic expectations.* Poor teachers are the "forgiving" and "understanding" ones who permit students to come to class late because "that's just the way those people are." The function of school is to set attainable goals for all students to meet. Members of minority groups expect and appreciate realistically high standards being set by teachers of their children.

7. *Sensitivity to differences in nonverbal messages.* Silence, lack of direct eye contact, and weak handshakes are examples of nonverbal communication which may be judged as negative behaviours in some cultures and as positive behaviours in others.

Finally, three fundamental principles should be kept in mind when teaching in multicultural classrooms.

1. Rely on proven teaching practices. Good practices in multicultural education often are good practices everywhere for everyone. These include paying special attention to cultural learning styles, knowing the students' home backgrounds, meeting personal needs, understanding the community, and communicating with parents. Although these practices are important in all teaching, they become critical in multicultural teaching situations.

2. Recognize academic ability and motivation. Multicultural education is not merely a matter of bringing recent immigrants and their children up to a "standard." Many immigrant children in the schools will be as academically talented and as motivated as the best North American students. Indeed, many of these students outperform their North American counterparts.

3. Education for many immigrant students may need to focus upon
   personal and interpersonal dimensions rather than academic factors.

YOUR PERSONAL INVENTORY OF "GOOD TEACHER" CHARACTERISTICS

Make a list of the characteristics of good teachers mentioned in this
chapter. Can you add to the list? Categorize these characteristics into
the columns in Figure 2.2. Place an asterisk beside items you particularly
want to work on.

Another approach is to make a list of your talents and interests.

FIGURE 2.2
PERSONAL CHARACTERISTICS FOR BEING A GOOD TEACHER

Things I have	Things I don't have	Things I'm not sure of

Chapter Three:

THE NATURE OF STUDENTS

Main Understandings

In this chapter you will learn the following:

1. To be effective, teaching methods must consider the nature of adolescents.
2. Good teaching balances the academic/knowledge aspect of learning and the values/feelings/creativity aspect.
3. Adolescents experience personal changes which influence their behaviour in school.
4. Students need to express themselves.
5. Students of different abilities and styles require different approaches in teaching.

The school years are a time of change and adaptation which extends far beyond merely sitting in a classroom and learning information taught by a teacher. A good teacher understands the nature of his or her students, and recognizes the personal things experienced by them.

Before adolescence — in the early grades — children tend to *want* to be obedient. They want to know the rules and are quick to report to the teacher anyone not following them. Elementary school children often actually *like* their teachers. They bring presents to their teachers occasionally. After school and at recess time they hang around to talk. For these kids, the teacher is often ranked number one.

In their teenage years they are suddenly loud, noisy, poking, pushing, wise-cracking, not watching what they are doing or where they are going as they walk about the schools. They're all dressed alike, with the disgusting sloppiness that adults deplore. They chatter about the same deafening rock groups. They groan in unison about their teachers and their homework. They worry about the same nest-leaving struggles with their parents. They all yearn for attention. Their skin colour differs; their size differs. They seem to be on an emotional roller coaster. They annoy any adult around them. They can drive their teachers crazy. But they're amusing to watch. They are noisy, self-preoccupied, young.

Although they are highly individualistic, they are a single group. They are a clan. They are members of the same big human family — students.

LEARNING STYLES

As illustrated in Figure 3.1, people learn by various means— observation, listening, manipulation, logical analysis, and intuition. Individuals tend to learn more effectively in one way than another. Some are predominantly logical thinkers; others may be very good at manipulating physical objects and numbers (experiential learning); yet others may be intuitive or creative thinkers. Each style has its special strengths. Students tend to do better when their teacher's learning style is similar to their own than when it is different. Teachers need to vary in their teaching to accommodate and adapt to students' learning styles.

Figure 3.1 portrays five different learning styles. Some people learn best by listening or observing, whereas others learn best by rolling up their sleeves and physically manipulating things. Some prefer to logically analyze the details of the situation; others prefer to learn within the context of emotional and intuitive experiences. Utilize your knowledge of learning styles by doing the following: First, identify the key elements of the various learning styles of students in your class. Second, match these styles to the organizational nature of the content and methodology in your classroom. Here are some contrasting learning styles you need to adapt to your students.

CONTRASTING LEARNING STYLES

Holistic/global versus Detailed/analytical

Some people tend to look at the big picture. They see the whole rather than the parts. Other people focus on details. They see the intricacies of the parts.

Figure 3.1
Dimensions of Learning Styles

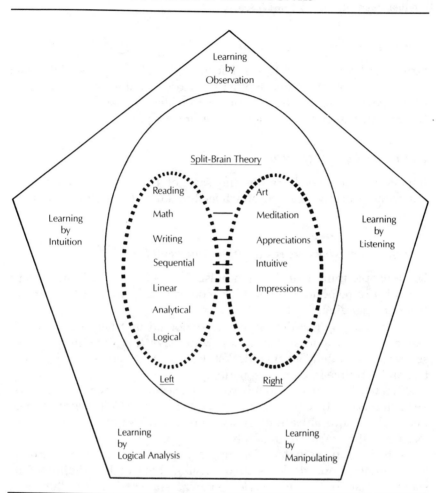

Experiential/concrete versus Abstract/theoretical

Abstract/theoretical thinkers focus on ideas and principles. They tend to philosophize and to think creatively. They prefer to manipulate ideas rather than things. Experiential/concrete thinkers like to do things and manipulate objects. They learn from experience. They need to see the relationship between the idea and the reality of the here and now.

Sequential versus Dispersed versus Cyclical

Sequential learners prefer to learn things in logical sequence. They like linear patterns, logic, flow charts, and sequential steps. Dispersed learners are capable of absorbing ideas like a sponge absorbs water. A particular sequence is not necessary. Others see ideas in a circular and cyclical fashion rather than linearly.

Structural versus Developmental

Structural learners need to see a structure — all the parts of the idea and how they relate to one another — before meaningful learning takes place. Developmental thinkers prefer to generate ideas first and allow the structure to evolve as the thinking process progresses.

Impersonal versus Affective

Impersonal thinkers learn for the sake of learning. The content is important. Affective learners attach feelings and attitudes to things they learn.

Intuitive/impulsive versus Cognitive/judgmental

Some people think quickly on impulse. They like to play hunches and are quick to respond. Others think more carefully, weighing all factors before responding.

These thinking/learning styles need not be mutually exclusive. A classroom may contain students who have cognitive/judgmental, sequential, and detailed/analytical styles. Other students may be affective and intuitive/impulsive in nature.

Often teachers fail to recognize diverse learning styles. Students have been stereotyped as inferior, non-creative, or dull simply because their personal or cultural learning styles were not the same as those of the teacher or the organization of the curriculum.

Try to identify your own learning style. Identify different learning styles among your students by observing them or by administering standard tests on learning styles. Analyze students' work. When and why was it successful or not successful? Under what conditions do some students learn better? Note their preferences about learning.

Survival of the species has depended on diversity; therefore, it follows that teachers must provide for the diversity of each student's learning style. They must provide diversity in methods, activities, and materials in their classrooms. Excellence, creativity, and intelligence come in many different forms.

SPLIT-BRAIN THEORY

Research based on brain disease and accidents indicates that the brain is in effect two separate organs joined by nerve tissue which integrates the functions of each half of the brain. Each hemisphere carries out separate physical, perceptual, and consciousness functions.

The right hemisphere controls the left side of the body and the left hemisphere controls the right side of the body.

As illustrated in Figure 3.1, split-brain theory holds that the left hemisphere specializes in linear, sequential, and logical thinking. Language development is largely handled by the left hemisphere, as are other linear functions such as reading, writing, and mathematical computation.

The right side of the brain controls other functions which are simultaneous in nature, including non-verbal thought, impressions, and appreciative and creative thought. The right hemisphere is active in art activities and meditation.

Split-brain theory may explain why some students excel in mathematics but are weak in English, while the reverse holds true for others.

Teachers need to include strategies which enable students to stimulate both hemispheres of the brain

---

The school system has traditionally emphasized activities of the left hemisphere. Today, educators are more aware of the importance of the right hemisphere, and schools do more interdisciplinary and thematic teaching and offer more instruction in areas such as music and art. Balance is key in the school curriculum, and teachers, regardless of the subject, need to provide stimulation for both sides of the brain.

If you have some understanding about the learning styles of your students, your teaching can be more effective

---

MEETING STUDENTS' NEEDS

Maslow (1968) pointed out that people's basic physical and emotional needs must be met before they can work on fulfilling more abstract needs (see Figure 3.2). This hierarchy of needs operates in the classroom. It is difficult to teach a hungry student how to calculate a mathematical formula. Students worried about conflicts at home or with their peers after school will have difficulty concentrating on their schoolwork.

FIGURE 3.2
MASLOW'S HIERARCHY OF NEEDS

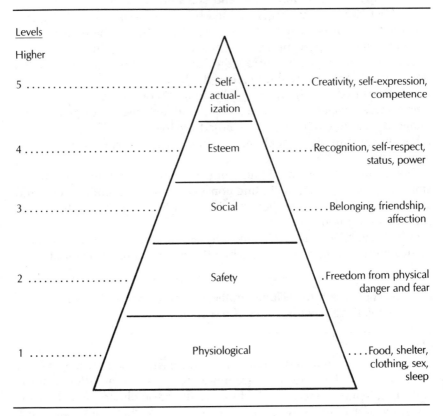

Levels

Higher

5 .... Self-actual-ization .... Creativity, self-expression, competence

4 .... Esteem .... Recognition, self-respect, status, power

3 .... Social .... Belonging, friendship, affection

2 .... Safety . Freedom from physical danger and fear

1 .... Physiological .... Food, shelter, clothing, sex, sleep

Source: Maslow (1968).

Good teachers try to recognize the various levels of needs in their students. No matter how good a lesson you have planned, it won't be effective if your students are unable to learn it because something else is bothering them or is a higher priority.

Some lessons may need to focus on needs other than academic — peer influences, self-respect, money problems, parent problems, etc. — before students can concentrate on academic learning.

Teachers cannot avoid these considerations. Hunger and clothing needs of students can be seen in schools. Accommodation may become an acute problem — for example, some students may be turned out of their homes temporarily. Physical and verbal abuse occurs in some households. The basic needs must be met before meaningful learning can occur in any classroom.

ADOLESCENTS' DEVELOPMENTAL TASKS

Psychologists Robert Havighurst and P.H. Dreyer (1975) described several "developmental tasks" that adolescents must learn to cope with: acceptance of one's physique, interest in the opposite sex, acquiring a set of values and an ethical system, and preparation for a career.

Acceptance of one's physique. Growth rates range widely within this age group. Girls may be taller than boys. Sports teams must contend with some students who are the size of adults and others who have not yet matured physically much beyond their elementary school years. Some students excel at sports while others lose interest in them.

Adolescents seem to spend more time gazing at themselves in the mirror than at the printed word in their textbooks. They continually run in and out of the school washrooms to check and double-check their hair, their makeup, their fingernails, their pimples, and their clothes.

Interest in the opposite sex. Again, the ranges are extreme. Some adolescents are preoccupied with the opposite sex and others show practically no interest. Girls tend to mature before boys, and this can result in girls being interested in and dating boys in higher grades, although this often is tempered by older boys' awareness that showing too much interest in girls in lower grades may not be socially acceptable within their peer group. Consequently, it can appear that the girls are chasing the boys rather than vice versa.

Every good teacher is a counsellor. These teachers are aware of their students — they can perceive special needs or concerns. They know when to seek special help and provide referrals.

Values and ethics. To acquire a set of values and an ethical system that will guide them to socially responsible behaviour, students need to explore and test various values. To their teachers, it can appear that students are always challenging the rules. But this rule-testing is the only way young people can formulate their code of acceptable conduct.

Preparation for a career. Even as they near the end of high school, many students do not know what they want to do or become. This, together with the increasing pressure for higher grades in order to enter some form of post-secondary education can cause them considerable anxiety.

At every level, teaching means more than just delivering effective lessons in the classroom

---

EARLY YEARS OF SECONDARY SCHOOL

Many teachers fail to recognize the maturity level and exploratory stages of their students. This problem is especially prevalent in schools in which Grades 7-9 are combined with high school. Teachers can easily fall into the trap of placing high-school expectations on junior high or middle-school students. This can make teachers unnecessarily frustrated and students unnecessarily anxious.

Know your students and accept them where they are

Students in Grades 5-9 are usually about 11-15 years of age. This group has several common characteristics.

They are confused by self-doubt, unsure of their position in their peer group and in life. They are forgetful, often leaving their books in their lockers and their assignments or their lunch at home.

Fads are a major influence, in clothes, hairstyles, and music. These youngsters are readily stimulated by mass media. They go crazy over certain music and crazier if they can make it to the live rock concert. If not, they'll make do with blaring music over the PA system at school dances. They can spend hours listening to music in their room or watching rock videos on TV.

Often these students are both passive and active. They can drift in daydreams or explode with bursts of energy. They are bored by routine and can respond with uncontrolled enthusiasm to something different.

Middle-years students are a terrific bunch to teach if you can understand them and be flexible but firm. Some teachers would not go near this group if their lives depended on it. Others would not trade them for what they perceive to be the more childish elementary-school students or the maturer but more placid students in the senior high school.

Military generals have said "Know thine enemy." Business entrepreneurs say "Know the competition." The same basic rule applies to teachers: "Know your students."

Figure 3.3 presents a summary chart of student characteristics and implications for teachers of middle-school students. Although these characteristics and implications for teaching are more readily apparent in the middle school, they apply to students in elementary and high school as well.

Add your own ideas to the list by considering the implications for teaching in particular subjects.

FIGURE 3.3
CHARACTERISTICS OF MIDDLE-YEARS STUDENTS AND THEIR IMPLICATIONS FOR TEACHERS

Student Characteristics	Implications for Teachers
PHYSICAL Wide variations in physical growth. Glandular imbalances. Sexual maturity. Ravenous appetites.	Act as a counsellor as well as a teacher. Offer adaptive Phys Ed classes. Avoid intense sports competition. Emphasize intramurals. Schedule classes in sex education, health, and hygiene. Allow snack times between meals. Include guidance on nutrition and personal body care.
SOCIAL Social development shifts from a family base to a peer base. Family values may remain influential, but family breakdown and mobility creates anxieties. Drastic behaviour at times — boisterous, aggressive, argumentative.	Communicate with the family. Organize school social/co-curricular activities to develop interpersonal relations and behaviour standards. Establish clubs and interest classes; use the buddy system.
"Puppy love" — changing infatuations; same-sex affiliations still dominate.	Role play. Offer social interaction opportunities through games and class parties. Large group events.
Group-oriented fads, materialism.	Student government, class discussion, group projects.
EMOTIONAL Emotional inconsistencies. Range in feelings. Real and imagined fears.	Encourage self-evaluation. Study options of behaviour and their consequences. Class atmosphere of friendliness, concern, and group cohesiveness.
Chemical and hormone imbalances trigger unexplained emotions.	Provide opportunities to release emotional stress. Don't pressure students to explain emotional outbursts.
Sensitive to criticisms of personal shortcomings.	Avoid sarcasm. Offer readings on people's personal problems to see that many problems are not unique.
INTELLECTUAL Intellectual development ranges from concrete manipulation to abstraction.	Individualization and flexible skill groupings.
Prefer active rather than passive learning activities. Interaction with peers.	Hands-on class activities. Avoid long periods of passive work.
High curiosity level. Egocentric.	Group discussions, learning centres, creative dramatics.
Some evidence of the slowing of brain growth among many 12-14-year-olds.	Teach real-life concepts of conflict, competition, peer influence. Community studies. Refine the cognitive requirements.

WHAT DO STUDENTS THINK?

Understanding your students' concerns helps your teaching. Students worry about what goes on at school: things like grades, not understanding the work, and interactions with teachers and other students. They are also frequently concerned about social and family situations (which undoubtedly affect school life): after-school time, money, sex, and parents' marriage(s). Self-consciousness causes other worries — about looks, height or weight, loneliness, and self-worth.

Figure 3.4 illustrates the complexity of students' concerns when they ponder their place in the world.

What will you do to make school a "good" place?

Pressure gets to everyone, including your students. If they experience pressure at home, pressure in their social lives, and money pressures, then school pressures such as unsuccessful completion of assignments can become a heavy load. The pressure to achieve high grades or earn money, or both, has taken a lot of the fun out of high school.

Sports and social activities have declined in many high schools because students spend more time studying or working at part-time jobs

---

For some students, a job is an economic necessity. Others work in order to maintain their lifestyles of cars, girlfriends or boyfriends, drugs, and new clothes. Either way, the job may cost them dearly in terms of school achievement.

Some students are strongly affect by alcohol — either by their personal consumption or through use by family members. National surveys have shown that nearly two-thirds of all teens have used alcohol on a regular basis, and more than 80 percent have experimented with it before age 12! Alcohol-related traffic accidents kill about 400 teenagers per year across Canada.

Some students simply cannot cope with the pressures they experience. In Canada the suicide rate among teenagers has jumped 400 percent since 1970. Teachers who listen to students may hear the cries for help that precede suicide.

One teacher can have tremendous influence on a student, and that one teacher may be the only bright light that the student can see. Many

FIGURE 3.4
A Student's Concerns

young students get more enjoyment from friends and music than from their families. For some, school replaces the family to some degree.

Young people have a strong need to express themselves. One way they do so is through their choice of music. Listen to the music your students play and try to figure out what it is saying. Sometimes these messages can be used to stimulate class discussions.

The good teacher achieves balance between teaching content, skills, and values in their lessons and paying attention to the personal needs and characteristics of the students

---

Teaching Students with Different Abilities

More and more students with special needs are being integrated into schools. You may have students in your classes who are mentally or physically handicapped or emotionally disturbed. Special adjustments must be made for these students.

The first rule is to get to know your students. Initially a teacher tends to see a class as one homogeneous group. Only after time and conscious effort do we begin to see the students as individuals. Begin by learning the names of your students. Practise your listening skills. Be sympathetic to what they tell you.

Every good teacher is a counsellor too

THE LEARNING-DISABLED

Teachers often are frustrated in working with students with learning disabilities, partly because most teachers have not experienced learning difficulties themselves and thus find it difficult to empathize with those who are struggling to learn. Sometimes the brightest people do not make the best teachers. If you have to struggle to learn difficult concepts, you can better understand those students who are experiencing similar difficulties. These students tend to respond very positively to personal attention.

Such students may lack spark. They may fail to participate in class. They may be the last to open their books and the first to forget their materials. They may follow directions poorly and often do not seem to understand their assignments. They may be incapable of recalling details and facts, and unable to relate these facts to principles.

Learning difficulties are not always caused by lack of intelligence. For example, the school system has sometimes branded students as slow learners when poor eyesight or poor hearing was the problem. Students may also be afflicted with more acute disabilities such as neurofibromatosis, cleft lip and palate, Downs syndrome, congenital heart defects, and fetal alcohol syndrome.

It is essential that teachers acquire some understanding of disabled children in order to accommodate their needs and help them achieve their individual maximum potential.

No student should be ignored, including the slower and more quiet ones. Requiring these students to do extra homework or serve work detentions will not help them to perform better.

A major error is to channel these students into the dumping-grounds within the school system, such as make-work programs. Students are assigned to these programs in order to get them out of the classroom and away from the teacher. These programs, ideally planned to provide work experiences for students, too often are dead-end streets.

If you have students with special needs, get to know them and accept them. These students need small tasks for success. They may have short attention spans and require more from the teacher. The material being taught needs to be adjusted to their needs — for example, the teacher might replace the textbook with short readings or simplify basic math problems.

These students require individual help and monitoring. Involve them in the class and school through various activities such as running errands, keeping score and keeping time, organizing classroom bookshelves and bulletin boards, and helping to set out and put away materials. Provide them with concrete experiences by using community resources, role-playing, and audiovisual material so they can better see the connections between what is being taught and the real world.

Co-operative learning in groups helps these students. Students can be encouraged to help each other through tutoring, showing, and coaching.

Teachers need to display a sympathetic and understanding attitude. Conduct individual interviews to help these students do their personal best.

Give assignments that students can complete successfully. Use oral assignments and testing, in addition to written forms. Ensure that sufficient time is allowed for students to complete and experience success with school tasks.

STUDENTS OF HIGH INTELLIGENCE

These students are fast finishers. They may also become your greatest discipline problem if they are bored or sense some form of injustice.

They are sensitive to peer pressure, articulate, and argumentative.

With these students, the teacher should be a resource provider rather than an individual monitor. If these students are provided with adequate resources, they will rise to the challenge on their own. They become frustrated quickly if told to wait and follow lockstep approach as the rest of the class may need to do. In order to challenge high achievers, give them questions and assignments requiring higher levels of thinking. Enrichment activities can be incorporated into activity centres in elementary school classrooms and in learning stations in the higher grades.

Because these students can handle the cognitive content of school-work so easily, the affective side of their education is sometimes neglected. Teachers should provide opportunities for co-operative projects and interchanges among students so they can practise leadership skills, and encourage decision-making, self-direction, and self-appraisal.

CREATIVE STUDENTS

Creative students see shortcuts, use fantasy and daydreaming a great deal, and have a bizarre or unique sense of humour. They are usually, but not always intelligent. They can be very mischievous, particularly if bored.

To teach creative students, the teacher must be flexible in letting things get done in more than one way. Personal projects should be encouraged. Classes should emphasize "how" and "why" questions so that various possibilities can be explored. Constructive criticism should be encouraged. Teaching creative students can become a running battle if a teacher attempts to force too many set patterns of behaviour and fails to recognize the individuality of students within the classroom.

ADJUSTING TEACHING TO LEARNERS' LEVELS

The overlapping triangles in Figure 3.5 illustrate how needs and abilities differ between students of higher intelligence and those of lower intelligence, and how teachers need to adjust their teaching approaches accordingly. Slower-learning students, represented in triangle *ABC*, require a great deal of teacher direction, repetition, and motivation. Their attention span, ability to remember, and creativity is more limited than that of higher-ability students.

In contrast, highly intelligent students, represented in triangle *DFE*, require greater freedom and opportunity to direct their own learning.

FIGURE 3.5
ADJUSTING TEACHING TO LEARNERS' LEVELS

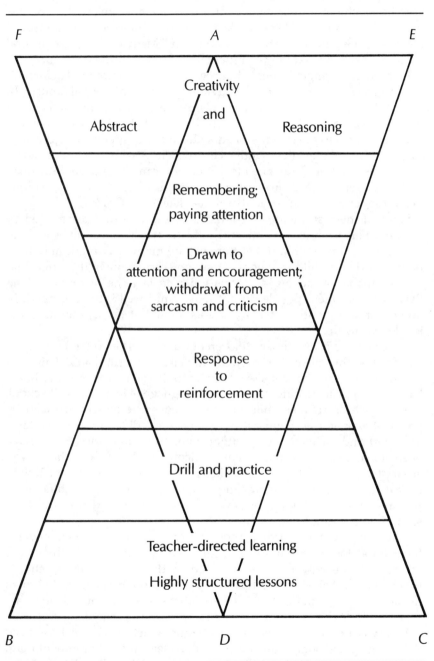

STUDENTS IN POVERTY

One in six children in Canada comes from a family below the poverty line, and Canada has been ranked second among eight westernized nations in the percentage of "poor children." Many of them live in rural areas, in the North, and in the inner cities.

In many cases anger is these children's overriding emotion. Their anger is manifested in aggressive behaviour, silence, or verbal abuse. In different ways they tell you "I'm ugly, I'm stupid, and my life is going nowhere, so don't tell me things are good, or that I am good. I will not believe you." These students need self-esteem desperately, and a way to begin to get their lives under control. They need to be listened to — they need a hug. They need teachers who can be satisfied with small and infrequent rewards from their profession. To get a smile or a simple hello from one of these students can feel like a great success.

Some of these students are confused by the way they are treated by teachers. For example, an eight-year-old who acts like an adult by looking after three younger children at home alone night after night may then be treated like a child at school. We assume erroneously that this child is not capable of making decisions when in fact she or he is making decisions that most people do not make until well into adulthood. In other instances, a student is treated as a child at home, but at school is told "Grow up."

Other factors characterize children of the poor. They often move back and forth within the city or between the city and a rural area. This high mobility can result in inconsistent attendance at school. Some have home languages which are different from the language of instruction at school. A few, such as refugee children, have been severely traumatized by personal experiences. Some are caught between different value systems at school and at home. Some suffer emotional difficulties. Some have been abused. Some are dependent on alcohol or drugs. Some have even attempted suicide. Often they live in a home environment in which their parents or guardians are struggling with the same emotional difficulties. As a result, many children in poverty lack a vision of the future. They see only today, not tomorrow.

Like any parent or guardian, those who are raising children in poverty have hope for their children's futures and want to help them. But although some may be very involved in their community's schools, others may feel alienated or hostile toward school because of their own negative school experiences. Teachers must show that "our" schools are "their" schools by involving the community in the school.

In any educational system, the classroom teacher is critical. We need to operate classrooms which are positive learning environments and include aesthetic human experiences. There needs to be a lot of talking and listening. We need to integrate concrete and practical elements into the math and physical science programs. Continuous learning assessment with detailed records and examples of students' work is required. Techniques of observation need to be practised in the evaluation system.

But one teacher alone cannot do the whole job, nor can one school. It takes an entire community team of teachers, school administrators, social workers, police (not for enforcement but for positive help), counsellors, home-school workers, special-project workers (for language and cultural programs, food programs, etc.), and parents. For students in poverty, the school becomes the centre of the community.

We must believe that something can be done. Many Canadian schools are filled with students who are tough, scarred, and poor — but in these schools, hope still flourishes.

The following are some examples of what schools with a population of children who live below the poverty line can do.

1. Offer an integrated unit in the world of work. Students can be scheduled to work at volunteer jobs to acquire a work ethic.
2. Bring in guest speakers to serve as role models.
3. Have older students "adopt" younger students and show them basic skills such as understanding bus schedules, how to read newspaper ads, and how to be better consumers. In a buddy system (or "school twins" or "care partners"), older students are paired with younger students to read to, talk to, and do things with them.
4. Develop a "special friends" program in which students are paired with people in daycare centres, seniors' homes, or convalescent homes and spend time with them.
5. Run a small business in the school — for example, a nutrition program in an elementary school, a Meals on Wheels project, a lunch program for school staff and special meetings, or the school cafeteria program. Students should be involved in all stages of planning and delivering the program, including time schedules, work responsibilities, and financial management.
6. Participate in craft projects at the school in areas such as woodwork, pottery, painting, sewing, etc.
7. Run support groups for students, such as special-interest clubs, coffee clubs, a parent support group, a self-awareness group, an anger-management group, a social-skills group, or a prenatal discussion group. Attendance should not be compulsory, and students should have the opportunity to set the agenda with advice from teachers. Students in poverty often have low self-esteem, and these groups provide much-needed support. Some teachers have to be willing to take a few extra students in their classes so others can be free to help run the special-needs groups.

Many students in community and inner-city schools often say that their teachers care for them. In contrast, in other schools they attended, too often teachers appeared to pay attention only to the smart or good students. When asked "How would you describe a good teacher?" one inner-city student responded:

> It is someone who will take time out of their own life to help you. This personal dimension is important. You can talk to them — carry on a conversation with them. They aren't hassling you with questions like "Why are you doing this?" You feel you can come up to them and talk. Teachers are more friends than authority figures. Schoolwork is important and is the vehicle, but personal feelings and a person's life has to get straight.

In these teaching situations the lecture approach is less effective. Hands-on and tutoring-type activities are better. Reading to the students is beneficial. Response journals, brief question-and-answer periods, making posters, and a lot of group work, group projects, and co-operative learning are effective in many instances.

How do you handle the problems of anger and aggressiveness? To yell or lash out is the worst thing a teacher can do. You may win the battle this way, but you will not win the war. Avoid overreacting. Other students realize that bursts of anger happen. Avoid isolating students in the classroom because it only makes them angrier. Don't take their anger personally; it is not directed at you, although it may seem like it in the heat of the moment. There are times when students explode and lash out at the nearest thing that represents the source of many of their frustrations, and this may happen to be the nearest teacher. Have a thick skin and you can bounce back to help them again.

If violence is a problem in the school, teachers must do their best to ensure a safe environment for students. Non-traditional approaches to classroom management (see Chapter 11), such as the logical consequences model, work best. In particular, students should not be suspended if it can be avoided. Suspensions serve the needs of teachers more than the needs of students. Above all, teachers must continue to be optimistic and believe in themselves and in their students.

Remember that these students also have dreams and aspirations. They want to become engineers, doctors, teachers, etc. Don't tell them that their expectations are unrealistic. It only dampens their hopes. Anyway, you might have underestimated their capabilities.

Humour is an essential ingredient. Not seeing the funny side or being negative can cause a teacher to burn out quickly. Take the attitude that there is humour in almost everything, and it can make teaching students of poverty very rewarding.

Chapter Four:
THE CURRICULUM

MAIN UNDERSTANDINGS

In this chapter you will learn the following:

1. The curriculum can be defined in different ways.
2. Both the formal and hidden curriculum must be taken into account in teaching.
3. The principles which underlie the curriculum are parallel to principles we must consider in our daily teaching.

The primary component in the school is the *student body*, consisting of individuals with a wide range of beliefs, attitudes, skills, and knowledge. Other parts of the school are *resources* such as the school building, books, papers, desks, computers, nets, balls, science and art equipment, and audiovisual aids, and the *school administration* and *staff members* such as caretakers, special assistants, consultants, secretaries, and teachers.

The *community* plays a significant role in the school. It has expectations concerning what and how children ought to be taught. Another essential component of the school is the *curriculum*, which we will discuss in this chapter.

All of these components influence every classroom teacher. Teaching is not merely an interaction between a teacher and students. It involves interaction and communications between teachers and several other bodies, all of which the teacher must contend with in order to achieve the ultimate goal of the school — the education of students.

What Is the Curriculum?

The school curriculum is a plan which provides guidance to teachers. It is a set of defined learning experiences for students. A curriculum guide exists for each subject in each of the grades.

The school curriculum ought to reflect the goals of the school program, which ideally include personal development for students in the following areas:

1. intellectual
2. social
3. emotional
4. physical
5. artistic

The curriculum guide defines the subjects which are to be taught and offers a rationale for teaching them.

The curriculum provides an overview of *content* to be taught — the main ideas — and suggests organizing *topics* and *themes*. It also offers suggestions on *how to teach* particular topics, and it recommends *evaluation* methods.

Guides are usually general in nature, and it is necessary to plan specific lessons or units to teach in the classroom. Teachers often make little use of curriculum guides once they have become familiar with the course of study and have had some experience in teaching the course. Teachers must breathe life into the curriculum guides.

In the past, many curriculum guides have been less than helpful — too brief, too vague, not user-friendly. They were based on the notion of local input into what was taught in schools. Often, however, it is impossible to translate the "community will" into precise classroom teaching objectives.

If teachers had read, understood, and practised the philosophy of method behind many old curriculum guides, we might not be experiencing changes in curriculum to the same extent today. Instead teachers relied on old practices rather than implementing new approaches advocated in the guides. Recent developments in curriculum have attempted to overcome some of these criticisms.

The curriculum is sometimes seen narrowly in terms of materials. But the curriculum should be more than a textbook or workbook. Such books can be a major component of the curriculum, but students should not be limited to learning only what is in one text. Teachers ought to incorporate into the curriculum updated information and activities designed to teach information and skills beyond those presented in one particular book.

INSTRUCTIONAL METHODS AND STRATEGIES

Instructional methods and strategies are a major part of the curriculum. Each subject can be taught in several basic ways. What are the strengths and weaknesses of each method? How should a particular topic be taught?

Ideally, a teaching method should be selected based on what is best for the students. Other factors, however, come into play, such as the teacher's own level of knowledge, availability of materials, the background of students (age, maturity, intelligence, abilities, interests, and motivation), and the purpose you wish to accomplish.

The school curriculum may be designed to develop *competencies and skills*. Focus is on process rather than content. Emphasis may be on social interaction process in social studies, the scientific method in chemistry or physics classes, or a life-long learning orientation to physical education. Content is not ignored, but greater attention is given to how things are learned. Knowledge is used as a stepping stone to acquire skills which can then be adapted and applied to new learning.

The curriculum can also focus on aspects of *community life* and *social action* — the real world — within which the student must learn to adapt and operate. Such a view of curriculum involves an understanding of society with its many technological and interpersonal demands and expectations.

THE FORMAL CURRICULUM AND THE HIDDEN CURRICULUM

The formal curriculum consists of the school subjects and academic skills. However, students learn many things in school that are not taught as part of the formal curriculum. This "hidden" curriculum comprises the informal and life skills which are learned from the interactions among students and between students and the school.

Learning to work around and through the massive sets of rules that bind a school together is part of the hidden curriculum. Students learn that some clothes and hairstyles are acceptable and others are not. Grades influence social groups in the school. Everyone can identify the "skids," the "jocks," the "wimps," the "sucks," and the "brains" in a high school. Many kinds of learning occur on the elementary playground at recess time. Students discover they can get away with certain things with one teacher but not with another.

The hidden curriculum can be as powerful a learning force as the formal curriculum. It also draws students to the school. Even those who are failing in the formal curriculum will still have a powerful drive to keep coming to school because of learning experiences in the hidden curriculum. The fact that a student is not learning sufficiently in the formal curriculum does not mean that school is inappropriate or a waste of time for him or her.

Even though a teacher's foremost concern is to deliver the formal curriculum, the impact of the hidden curriculum on students cannot be ignored. The methodology of the hidden curriculum includes recognizing the influence of school rules on student behaviour. School social functions such as class parties, school dances, sports events, plays, and special awards must be assessed regularly. The hidden curriculum should be discussed openly in class, and examined and evaluated in terms of its impact on students' learning.

PRINCIPLES OF THE CURRICULUM

There are several principles which underlie the organization and structure of a curriculum. These principles are described in terms of the provincial curriculum, but they also apply to the planning of daily lessons.

SCOPE AND SEQUENCE

Sequence refers to the order in which topics are presented. It prevents overlapping and redundancy. It is very disappointing to be prepared to teach a topic and have your students exclaim "But we took that last year!"

Scope refers to the breadth or depth in which a topic is taught. The suggested units within each topic for each grade provide teachers with some guideline as to the breadth or depth in which a topic might be handled. If a teacher chooses to go into great depth or detail on a topic, it is only natural that the breadth of the topic becomes more narrow. For example, in teaching about the principles of flight, a teacher could focus in depth on how air travels over an airplane wing. This means that there would not be time to teach the principles of bird flight, the history of early airplane flights, or the principles of rocketry. Another teacher might choose to teach the topic from a broader base and study these other aspects of flight. There would not be the time to go into great depth on subtopics, but students would get a survey on a broader scale.

> **The broader the scope, the less depth or detail. The narrower the scope, the deeper or more detailed the topic.**

Teachers must decide on the breadth or depth in which they wish to teach topics to their class. This decision is based on a number of factors such as the needs of students, the time and resources available, the interests of the teacher and students, and the background and personal experiences of the teacher.

CONCRETE TO ABSTRACT

As they progress through the grades, students move from understandings nearer their experiences to knowledge about things which are more removed from them. In Mathematics, elementary students learn number concepts by physically manipulating blocks and sticks. By Grade 12 they are capable of solving algebraic formulas which are symbolic and abstract. In Physical Education, students first learn how to bounce the ball and throw baskets, then move on to practising more abstract aspects of the game of basketball such as the full-court press and the zone defence. In Science, younger students learn about their immediate environment, whereas older students manipulate formulas to determine various chemical and physical properties. Elementary students study concrete experiences in their local communities; high-school students study national and global issues.

To understand abstract ideas, students first need to grasp concrete principles to which they can relate the abstract information which is not yet within the realm of their experience.

SPIRAL CURRICULUM

Spiralling is based on the principle that you cannot teach everything to everyone at one time. Students may not grasp the ideas when they are first introduced, so the teacher returns to the skill or the information at a later date, and some students "catch on" or extend their understanding during the second or third time studying the material.

In Mathematics, students are initially introduced to the idea of numbers being represented by letters or symbols. After studying other aspects of math such as geometric figures, problem-solving, and numerals, students return to the idea of numbers being represented by symbols, and the concept of equations is introduced. A month or so later, equations are introduced again in greater depth, and students learn how to balance equations. At each focus on equations, students are required to learn about the topic in greater depth.

Principles of the curriculum are applicable in our daily teachings

---

In English or Language Arts, primary-school students are introduced to the formation of letters. Later, students learn that these letters are combined to form words, words are combined to form sentences, sentences are put together to form paragraphs, and paragraphs are linked to form essays.

In Geography, students are initially introduced to maps in terms of symbols and basic landforms. Later, the concepts of direction and scale are introduced. Other concepts, such as elevation, are then studied with the use of contour maps and stereograms.

THE CONCEPTUAL APPROACH

In the conceptual approach, topics are organized around main ideas, not isolated facts and details. Teachers ask "What is the most important thing my students should learn about this topic?" and focus on the answer to this question rather than on details. Accumulating facts is not an end in itself, but a necessary stage in the process of formulating major ideas (concepts) and conclusions or understanding (generalizations). In order to help students arrive at these major ideas, it is necessary to teach examples and *relevant* facts which build students' understanding of a topic.

BALANCE

The curriculum should be balanced in its content. Not all of Social Studies is history; it is balanced with other perspectives from Geography, Economics, Political Science, Sociology, and Psychology. Math is not calculations alone, but contains elements of problem-solving and application. A student's Science program contains both natural and physical sciences — Physics, Chemistry, Biology, Earth Sciences, and Astronomy. In some subjects, balance is struck between traditional and modern content. For example, in some English courses students study Shakespearean plays and modern novels, and in Social Studies, they may study selected periods of Canadian history as well as contemporary society and current world issues.

The curriculum must be broad as well as specific

The curriculum should also balance skills and values as well as knowledge.

FLEXIBILITY

To what extent should a teacher adhere to the curriculum as defined in the provincial curriculum guide? Should a teacher have the choice of teaching topics in the curriculum guide, topics of special interest to students, topics demanded by the local community, or topics outlined in the textbook?

The curriculum guide should be perceived as just that, a guide, not a set of inflexible rules or outlines of content carved in stone. If the official curriculum is too restrictive it hinders teachers from making curriculum decisions in the best interest of their students. On the other hand, if the curriculum is too broad or flexible, it fails to provide sufficient commonality and guidance for teachers. The curriculum attempts to be broad enough to offer variation and professional decision-making, but specific enough to provide some commonality and direction.

CURRICULUM CHANGE

School curricula in many provinces have been revised and updated to refocus students' learning to meet the demands of a changing society. The curriculum must reflect the larger educational and societal context in which young people must learn to cope and survive. Our society is progressing rapidly toward a postindustrial era characterized by an abundance of information, new communication technology, and closer contact among people on a global scale.

As a result, many former curriculum guides have required complete revision. Many topics are too complex to be covered in a single textbook. Differing values, conflicts between rich and poor nations, relationships between superpowers and small nations, and problems associated with the management of large governments when combined with technological advances on a global scale have brought new topics and issues into the school curriculum.

COMPULSORY SUBJECTS IN ELEMENTARY AND HIGH SCHOOL

English, Mathematics, Science, Social Studies, Health, Physical Education, and Art are frequently compulsory subjects.

The majority of class time is devoted to teaching these subjects. The remaining time may be devoted to other subjects approved by the Ministry of Education, such as a second language or Native Studies, which reflect the needs of individual communities.

The circle graph in Figure 4.1 indicates the amount of time typically devoted to various subjects during elementary and middle school.

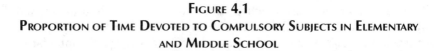

FIGURE 4.1
PROPORTION OF TIME DEVOTED TO COMPULSORY SUBJECTS IN ELEMENTARY AND MIDDLE SCHOOL

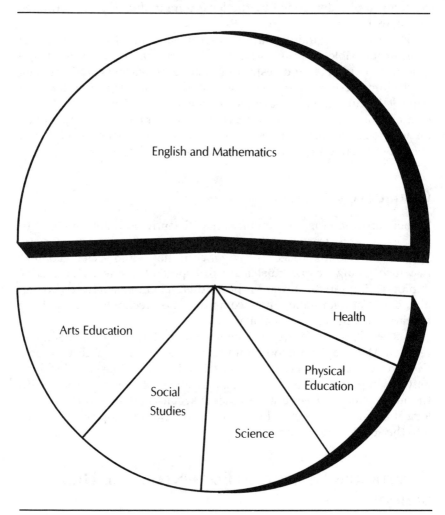

THE CURRICULUM IN PRIMARY YEARS

In the first few years of schooling, subjects are integrated, not taught in isolation. It is particularly critical in primary grades that teachers pay close attention to students' intellectual, emotional, social, physical, and aesthetic needs. Children must be allowed to inquire into matters of concern to them. Children learn through creative play with various materials such as crayons, chalk, dough, clay, scissors, puzzles, beads, blocks, and other materials.

The curriculum in primary years is organized and delivered in special ways, although it is important for teachers in the higher grades to recognize that these principles have merit throughout the K-12 curriculum. In primary classrooms whole-class instruction should be kept to a minimum. Most lessons should be geared to small groups or individuals. Flexible learning groups can be formed around special interests as well as academic needs.

In the primary classroom a variety of activities should progress simultaneously. They should be scheduled flexibly so that children of varying abilities have many opportunities to participate in group projects with teachers observing and recording. Children should be free to move about, converse, work together, and seek help from one another. They need opportunities to make decisions about their work and to develop responsibility for setting and meeting their educational goals. The curriculum is often delivered within a "multi-age activity" grouping where children work at different skill levels within the same classroom.

The focus is on children as learners. The learning begins from where the child is and moves forward as the child is able. This continuous learning model builds on the developmental levels of children and takes into account the fact that people learn at different rates and in different ways. Principles such as continuous progress, flexible scheduling, and individualization apply to all students. Although many of the above-mentioned principles of the primary curriculum are applicable to all grades, they are particularly important in teaching children in the early years of school.

ASSESSING YOUR CURRICULUM

The following checklist can help you evaluate the curriculum you are required to teach.

1. Does the curriculum adhere to the philosophy and structure established by the Ministry of Education?
2. Is it consistent with sound pedagogical theory and research?

3. Is the curriculum supported by a sufficient variety of materials and alternative teaching strategies for classroom teachers?
4. What strategies are in place to implement the curriculum in all schools?
5. Are the curriculum guides written clearly? Can they actually be used by all teachers?
6. Does the curriculum include a skills-development chart which provides guidance for teachers at various grade levels for introducing, reinforcing, and emphasizing particular skills?
7. Does the curriculum encourage teachers to relate the subject to the contemporary worlds of children, teenagers, and adults?
8. Does the curriculum provide opportunities for teachers to encourage students in critical thinking and higher levels of thought?
9. To what extent have various educational sources such as the professional teachers' organization, classroom teachers, and the university been involved in designing the curriculum?
10. Is there consistency between the philosophy of the curriculum and what is offered in teacher education programs?
11. Is there adequate guidance for the evaluation of student learning in each of the major areas of educational development — knowledge, skills, and values?

Part II:
PLANNING FOR TEACHING

Chapter Five:
WRITING
OBJECTIVES

MAIN UNDERSTANDINGS

In this chapter you will learn the following:

1. Teachers must write objectives in each of the areas of knowledge, skills, and values.
2. Learning objectives are more appropriate than behavioural objectives for planning most "normal" class lessons.
3. Learning objectives are appropriate for group or whole-class lessons. Behavioural objectives may be appropriate for individualized instruction, programmed learning packages, and writing individual test items.

Education must have a purpose. Specifically, the teacher must clarify the objectives for each lesson or unit. There will be objectives regarding each of knowledge, skills, and values. For example, even though students are acquiring knowledge in a particular lesson, the real purpose of the lesson could be to develop skills such as speaking and writing more effectively or working effectively as a member of a group. The well-taught class should enable students to practise such skills, as well as learning the content of the lessons.

Teachers also must encourage the development of students' values, attitudes, feelings, and beliefs, and give students opportunities to express their views about new ideas and issues.

What Is an Objective?

An objective is the purpose of a lesson. It is best determined from the point of view of the student: What will the student learn, or be able to do, as a result of the lesson?

Learning objectives are best written in the form of a direct statement focusing only on the most important points of the lesson.

Learning Objectives and Behavioural Objectives

Teachers must identify both learning objectives and behavioural objectives. (See Figure 5.1.)

Figure 5.1
Learning Objectives and Behavioural Objectives: A Comparison

Learning Objectives	Behavioural Objectives
1. For classroom/group instruction.	1. For individualized instruction and writing test items.
2. Describe the most important concept to be taught in the lesson.	2. Describe each student's observable behaviour in the learning situation.
3. Separate the learning (objective) from the doing (procedures and activities).	3. Equate observable behaviour with attaining the lesson's objective.
4. "The student will *learn* that. . . ."	4. "The student will be *able* to. . . ."

Learning objectives are designed for whole-class or group instruction and focus on the key concept to be taught. (Curriculum guides and teaching methods textbooks also use other terms synonymously with "learning objectives": major understanding, generalization, principle, key point, or main idea.)

Behavioural objectives are designed for individualized instruction and focus on observable behaviour. Although behavioural objectives can be written for most "regular" classroom teaching situations, they are often less appropriate than learning objectives. Many teachers (and university professors) do not write behavioural objectives for their courses.

Faculties of education often require student teachers to write behavioural objectives in their methods classes. But when these student teachers enter actual classroom teaching, they discover that the way in which they were instructed to write objectives does not quite fit with the lessons they must now plan and teach. An understanding of both behavioural and learning objectives, and their different purposes, is required for the clear and meaningful planning and teaching of lessons.

WRITING LEARNING OBJECTIVES

Four principles need to be kept in mind when writing learning objectives.

1. Ask yourself "What must the students learn in this lesson?"
2. Write the answer to this question in one straightforward and simple sentence.
3. In your lesson plan, separate what the students must learn from what they must do.
4. Clearly distinguish the *topic* from the *objective* of the lesson. Suppose, for example, that the topic is Canadian immigration patterns. Stating that your objective is "To learn about Canadian immigration patterns" is not very helpful. Instead, describe the most important point or principle. For example, you could write: "Less restrictive Canadian immigration patterns have led to an increase in the number of immigrants from Asia," if this were the most important point you wanted to make in the lesson. The remainder of the lesson plan would then consist of procedures, activities, and materials needed to teach this point.

   In general, a learning objective should begin with "The student will learn *that* ...," not "The student will learn *about*. ..."

A learning objective is the key point of a lesson

The following are examples of how to write learning objectives in various subject areas.

SOCIAL STUDIES

The three learning objectives listed below were written by a teacher who preferred to identify key points in *universal* terms.

Students will learn that:

1. It is possible for people to live simultaneously in two distinct worlds — ancient traditions and modern technology.
2. Rapid transportation and communication have made the various nations of the world increasingly interdependent.
3. The concentration of land and wealth in the hands of a few in Mexico created a polarized society between rich and poor.

   With the first learning objective, the teacher was able to draw examples from several cultures — Canadian aboriginal people, immigrants, and groups of people elsewhere in the world.

Match your objective with the rest of the lesson

The second learning objective enabled the teacher to illustrate the first with examples such as global satellite television networks, short-wave radio, jet aircraft, trans-oceanic ships, and international trade.

The third learning objective is more directly related to the particular topic — Mexico. It identifies the main idea that the teacher wants students to learn. Once this is done, the teacher can now proceed to plan the rest of the lesson in terms of materials, questions, activities, and seatwork.

PHYSICAL EDUCATION

A physical education teacher wants to teach students how to "set" a volleyball correctly. She would like students to set the ball 10 times without losing control of it.

A teacher thinking in terms of a behavioural objective for the lesson might write "The student will be able to set the ball a minimum of 10 times following the teacher's demonstration."

In contrast, a teacher thinking in terms of a learning objective will ask "What will the students have to *learn* in order to do this activity?" The answer to this question becomes the learning objective for the lesson. This key idea is the objective, and again, it is best written as a straightforward, direct sentence.

Thus, the objectives for the volleyball lesson could be:

The student will learn that:
1. The body must be proportionally balanced with knees bent and legs evenly spread.
2. Fingers must be cupped so the palm of the hand does not slap the volleyball.

These two objectives become the major focus. Unless students learn these two principles, they will not be able to accomplish the tasks of the lesson.

HEALTH

A teacher who wants to teach about eye ailments could write the following learning objective:

The student will learn that untreated cataracts can adversely affect vision.

This objective would enable a teacher to plan several class activities leading students toward understanding of this basic idea. For example, the concept of a cataract might be discussed with the class. The teacher might sketch a cataract on the chalkboard, noting how muscles in and around the eye affect the operation of the lens and pupil. The teacher could then discuss causes of cataracts (injury, extreme heat, radiation, disease, etc.) and how cataracts can be removed surgically.

AGRICULTURE

A teacher wants to teach a lesson about agriculture on the Canadian prairies. This lesson might include information on the advantages and disadvantages of fertilizers and chemicals in agriculture, climate changes caused by the greenhouse effect, and current farming practices.

The teacher might write the following learning objective:

The student will learn that the advantages of no-tillage farming practices for conserving soil moisture need to be weighed against the potential disadvantages associated with the increased use of chemicals to control weeds.

To achieve this objective, the teacher would first teach about the concepts of "conventional tillage" and "no tillage," noting the effects of each kind of plowing on soil moisture and erosion. Then a chart on the chalkboard would be used to illustrate the advantages and disadvantages of controlling weeds through chemical spraying.

By the end of the planning, the teacher realized that the students also needed to learn that:

The greater the tillage of the land, the greater the loss of soil moisture and increase in erosion.

This objective, combined with the first, provided a clear direction to the lesson.

This example illustrates the importance of initially writing your learning objective, planning the procedures and activities you will use to teach this objective, and finally checking to see that your objective fits the rest of your lesson. In this example, the teacher realized that another learning objective was appropriate for the lesson.

ENGLISH/LANGUAGE ARTS

Students in one class were to read a story in which the main character said one thing one day and another thing another day. This inconsistent behaviour created tensions and conflicts among other members of the character's family. The teacher wanted students to learn the following principle (the learning objective) from the story.

The student will learn that inconsistent behaviour can create confusion and conflict.

With this objective in mind, the teacher could use the story as an example of this idea. He or she could also refer to other examples (from students' personal experiences, conflicts between groups, national or global conflicts, etc.) to reinforce the basic idea of the lesson.

The teacher could also write the objective as follows:

James Dunn's inconsistent behaviour created conflict among other members of his family.

Because it limits the lesson's focus to James Dunn's particular behaviour, this objective is not quite as good as the first, which is more universal in nature. The first objective allows the teacher to use several examples, including the behaviour of the story's main character, to reinforce the basic idea.

SCIENCE

A teacher wants to teach about butterflies as part of a unit on insects. The teacher plans to have students learn the characteristics of butterflies, but does not want them to confuse butterflies with moths. For this lesson, it would be appropriate to write:

Students will learn that, although moths and butterflies belong to the same order of species, they have distinguishing characteristics.

Objectives set the direction for a lesson

Once this objective has been selected, the next step is to outline procedures and activities. For example, sorting cards which describe butterflies and moths might be used, with the characteristics of each summarized in a chart on the chalkboard.

The conclusions or principles drawn from classroom experiments in science are the learning objectives for many of these lessons. For example, a teacher planned to teach an experiment which showed that air expands when heated. The learning objective was:

The student will learn that air expands when heated.

An objective should define the most important thing to learn in a lesson

---

To teach this basic idea, the teacher performed an experiment in which air inside a balloon was heated, increasing the size of the balloon. Students observed the demonstration, recorded the procedures in the experiment, and concluded, as in the teacher's original objective, that air expands when heated.

Another science teacher wanted to teach about the extinct prehistoric horses which lived at one time on the grasslands of Europe and Asia. A learning objective should not focus on an isolated fact or detail, such as "Early horses had three toes on each foot and were smaller than modern horses." A learning objective such as "Horses have changed since early times," or better yet, "Living things have adapted and changed in order to survive" would be more appropriate. Such a learning objective provides a reason why it is worthwhile to study characteristics of early horses. It is not these characteristics *per se* that are important, but the fact that their evolution into those of the modern horse represent a principle of how and why living things adapt and change. Again, the underlying principle should be identified in your statement of the learning objective for your lesson.

MATHEMATICS

Suppose a teacher wants to design a math lesson to teach students to determine mathematical progressions. There were numerous exercises in the math textbook. A behavioural objective would identify what students must do (*e.g.*, correctly get seven out of ten of the exercises correct).

A learning objective will identify the key principle that students must learn before they will be able to do the exercises. Therefore, to teach about the topic "arithmetic progression" a teacher might write the following objective:

> The student will learn that, in an arithmetic progression, a constant number (represented by d) must be added to each number in order to identify the succeeding numbers in the progression.

If students fail to learn this fundamental aspect of arithmetic progressions, they will be unable to do the exercises. They will have failed to learn the objective (basic key idea) of the lesson.

In Grade 12 Algebra, the topic might be "trigonometric identities." The objective in the textbook was written in terms of students' behaviour: "To simplify trigonometric identities." For this lesson, the teacher would write two learning objectives:

> The student will learn that:
> 1. Pythagorean identities can be expressed as a difference of two squares.

2. The more complex side of the identity must be simplified until it is identical with the other side.

The teacher has decided that these two principles must be understood in order for students to achieve the objective outlined in the text (which was written in terms of student behaviour). The teacher asked the question "Which principles must students learn in order to successfully complete these activities?" The answer to this question, written in terms of the two principles noted above, becomes the learning objectives for this lesson.

WRITING OBJECTIVES IN TERMS OF ACTIVITIES

A common but less desirable approach to writing objectives is to write them in terms of activities that students will perform. These objectives are usually prefaced with the phrase "The student will be able to. . . ." For example:

> The student will be able to identify the reasons underlying the Métis rebellion in Saskatchewan.
>
> The student will be able to describe the differences between fusion and fission.

Another variation is to begin the objective with "To. . . ." Such an objective may be written in terms of either the student or the teacher. For example, a teacher might write the objective:

> To compute the area of a parallelogram.

The same objective can be written in terms of the teacher:

> To teach how to compute the area of a parallelogram.

Writing objectives in this manner indicates the general purpose of the lesson, but it fails to answer the ultimate question which must be answered in order to teach the lesson: "What must students learn in order to perform these activities?"

In the case of the objective "To calculate the area of a parallelogram," the question which must ultimately be answered is "What must the student learn in order to calculate the area of a parallelogram?"

The answer to this question is really the key point to the lesson. Unless students learn this point (about the area of a parallelogram) they will not be able to understand how the area of this geometric figure is calculated.

The real learning objective (what students must learn in order to do the calculation) becomes:

> The student will learn that a parallelogram is a special form of a rectangle and therefore its area can be calculated in a similar way to that of a rectangle.

If students learn or understand this principle (objective), they will be able to perform the activity (calculating the area of a parallelogram).

It is less helpful to write an objective only in terms of the lesson's topic. In the example of the lesson on the area of a parallelogram, the *topic* is "the area of a parallelogram." The *activity* is to calculate this area. The *objective* is the statement that tells what students must learn in order to do the calculation (that parallelograms are special kinds of rectangles).

WRITING BEHAVIOURAL OBJECTIVES

Behavioural objectives have received a great deal of attention in education. They describe a lesson's objective in terms of a student's behaviour — what the student will *do*, rather than what she or he will *learn*. These types of objectives combine the doing and learning into one statement.

Behavioural objectives were designed for individualized instruction and have four characteristics:

1. They are designed with the student in mind.
2. They describe observable behaviour.
3. They include conditions of performance.
4. They identify minimum criteria.

Examples include:

After observing an experiment, the student will be able to list at least four reasons for the paper turning blue.

After watching a film, students will describe at least two ways in which an offside infraction can occur in hockey.

The students will be able to orally describe their feelings toward the main character after reading the story "The Hawker's Return."

The strengths of behavioural objectives are that they (a) specify, in observable terms, what students will be able to do to show they have mastered the lesson content, (b) are useful in basic skill subjects, (c) clarify, to students, what expectations are to be met, and (d) are suitable for individualized instruction.

Chapter Six:
PLANS FOR TEACHING

Main Understandings

In this chapter you will learn the following:

1. Teaching requires both short-range and long-range planning — daily lessons, units, day plans, weekly timetables, and year plans.
2. It is especially important for new teachers to prepare lesson plans in detail.
3. Although a beginning teacher must have daily lesson plans clearly set out, experience enables a person to move from the lesson-plan level to the unit-plan level.
4. Unit plans need to be detailed enough that so teachers can draw from them to fill out the daily plan book and teach their lessons.
5. Long-range planning enables teachers to adjust and balance the subjects they teach.

The teacher who is well prepared will teach more effectively. If the teacher does not know what is going on in the classroom, students will feel lost and uncertain. Poor planning leads to discipline problems and anxiety on the part of both teacher and students.

A teacher must plan and organize on at least five levels:

1. lesson plans
2. unit plans
3. day plans
4. weekly timetables
5. year plans

The first plan a student teacher must develop is an individual lesson plan. After some experience in teaching from a lesson plan, student teachers are then required to develop unit plans. Once you begin to teach from your unit plan, you can fill out the day-plan book, drawing from appropriate sections of your unit plan.

If your unit plan is sketchy, you will still need to write individual lesson plans throughout the unit. However, if your unit plan has been developed in sufficient detail, it will be unnecessary to write individual lesson plans. You should be able to write up your day-plan book by drawing from your unit plan. This stage in your development as a teacher normally occurs in the latter stages of practice teaching. The weekly timetable is designed by elementary teachers or by the school administration in upper grades. It helps you plan for the time spent on various subjects during a week. Your year plan becomes important when you become a teacher with your own class for the whole term.

Lesson Plans

Student teachers are usually asked to set out their lesson plans in writing. This serves two purposes:

1. It helps you organize in detail exactly what you will do and say in the forthcoming lesson.
2. It provides an opportunity for other people, such as your college supervisor or supervising teacher, to discuss with you your ideas and organization for the lesson.

The amount of detail in a written lesson plan depends on the complexity of the lesson and on your own experience and background. In general, beginning practice teachers find it helpful to write out their plans in detail. More experienced teachers need fewer details in their lesson plans. It is critical that your initial lessons are thought through and written out in detail. Writing your lesson plan helps you organize your thoughts.

A lesson plan usually focuses on one class period. It may be only 10-15 minutes long or nearly a full hour. A lesson is usually taught in a single class period, but may spread over two or more classes. Although there are a number of formats for lesson plans, each of them requires the teacher to consider topics, material, objectives, procedures (introduction, steps, closure), and evaluation. The procedures in Chapter 7 will help in planning your initial lessons, particularly the "procedures" section of your lesson plan.

PARTS OF A LESSON PLAN

The lesson *topic* may be determined by the course, or a class project. Your supervising teacher might suggest a topic. You might decide on the topic for study on the basis of student interest, your own priorities, or some information available to you.

Consider the *material* needed for the lesson. Will the chalkboard need to be clear for some writing? Are the lab materials set out? Is a film projector available? Will students need microscopes, rulers, or books during the lesson? To avoid disruption of your lesson, be certain that all the materials you will need are on hand and in working order.

Objectives need to be clearly spelled out. What do you expect your students to get out of this lesson? Decide whether your main focus is on knowledge, skills, or values.

Select the manner in which you wish to state the objectives for your lesson. For most lessons it is recommended that you write *learning objectives* as these are more meaningful to most teachers. Think of your objective in terms of what is most important for students to learn — the key point.

It is important that you establish expectations common to yourself, your supervising teacher, and the college supervisor. It is also important that you feel comfortable in the way you write the objectives for the lesson you will be teaching.

The *procedures* section of your lesson plan should include introduction, main steps, and closing. First, think of how to begin your lesson in order to interest the class in what you will be teaching. Ways to begin a lesson include:

- Give directions.
- Provide an overview of what is going to happen.
- State your objectives.
- Review the previous lesson.
- Tell students what they will be doing in the lesson.

> **Good planning gives a teacher the confidence to be flexible**

Here are some ways to get the students interested in your lesson:

- Tell an interesting but brief story.
- Ask a question.
- Show pictures.
- Role-play.
- Show an object. –
- Play a guessing game.
- Refer to students' personal lives, attitudes, or ideas.
- Refer to a quotation.
- Relate some interesting facts.
- Demonstrate something interesting.

Second, list the things you will do in the lesson. Write out main guide questions and include potential or expected responses.

Third, consider how you will end the lesson. Don't break off abruptly in the middle of some point or activity; think of a way to wrap it up. This list offers some ideas.

- Summarize what was learned or done in the lesson.
- Have the students review by asking them a few main summarizing questions.
- Have students work at their desks in related follow-up work until the end of the period.
- The class discussion or sequence of questions addressed to students leads toward and arrives at the conclusion or solution to the topic or issue under discussion, or to the demonstration or experiment done during the class.

Finally, give some thought in your lesson plan to *evaluation*. There are two aspects of evaluation:

- Evaluation of the students.
- Your own evaluation of how well the lesson seemed to go.

The teacher might evaluate students by presenting an oral or written quiz near the end of the lesson. More frequently, she or he assesses students informally, considering such questions as "Did the class seem to be following me?" "How well did they respond to my questions?" "Did they pay attention?" "Could they do the follow-up work?"

To evaluate yourself, before teaching your lesson, identify something you want to achieve. Some examples might be "giving clear directions," "asking a logical sequence of questions," "asking questions beyond the simple memory-recall level," "involving most students in a discussion." Reflect on the identified area for improvement and talk it over with the supervising teacher or college supervisor who has watched you teach.

If you are not satisfied, work to improve the identified skill in your next lesson.

SAMPLE LESSON PLAN: THE OIL SLICK EXPERIMENT

Materials: oil, pails, sponge, string, detergent, paper towels, newspapers

Objectives: [Learning Objective] The students will learn that oil mixed in water is difficult to clean up and creates environmental problems.

[Behavioural Objective] The students will be able to identify at least three negative consequences of oil spills on the environment.

Procedures: A. Introduction (Motivational Set)
Ask "Have you ever heard the expression 'Water off a duck's back?'" Read handout about the Arctic oil spill.

B. Main Steps and Key Questions
1. Explain how to set up the experiment.
   a) Put students into assigned groups. Ask "What do you think will happen when you pour the oil onto the water?"
   b) Pour oil into oil pails.
   c) Try the various clean-up techniques. Ask "Which materials were most effective for cleaning up the oil? How would you dispose of the oil-soaked clean-up materials?"
   d) Pour liquid detergent onto the oil slick. Ask "What happened? Why did the oil and detergent separate?"

C. Closing
1. Ask concluding questions: "How would you predict which material would clean up the oil best? Where do you think the oil would go in the ocean? How would it affect sea life? How would birds and land animals be affected? How would professionals clean up a real oil spill on the ocean?"
2. Follow-up Assignment
Ask students to put boiled eggs in a container of oil overnight, predict what will happen, and remove the shells from the eggs next day and report what happened.

D. Evaluation
1. Student Evaluation
Did students follow the procedures in doing the experiment? Could students respond to the key questions throughout the lesson? Could students identify three negative consequences of oil spills on the environment?
2. My Teaching Performance
Were my directions for doing the experiment clear? Was my classroom management effective when students were doing the experiment?

Unit Plans

During the practicum, student teachers often must teach several units, depending on various factors such as grade level, subject, and nature of the class or school situation. The following six questions will help teachers organize unit plans.

1. What is a unit plan?
2. Why teach from a unit plan?
3. When should a unit plan be organized and taught?
4. How long should a unit be?
5. How is a unit plan organized?
6. What is the relationship between lesson plans, unit plans, and the day-plan book?

WHAT IS A UNIT PLAN?

A unit plan organizes teaching around a central topic or theme. Although making individual lesson plans is the first concern of a student teacher, after some teaching experience it soon becomes necessary to prepare units of work. A well-designed unit is a classroom action plan that clarifies both purpose and procedures for teaching over the next several days or weeks. A unit plan is *not* a sequence of individual lesson plans.

WHY TEACH FROM A UNIT PLAN?

With several grades and class subjects to teach, it is unrealistic to plan lesson by lesson only one day ahead of the students. Teaching from a unit plan enables teachers to enjoy some breathing room from daily plan preparation. They can then take some time to think about what they are doing from a broader perspective, and reflect on teaching in the three major areas of educational development — knowledge, skills, and values. All of these objectives may not come into focus during every lesson, but over the longer perspective of a unit, each area should be part of every student's educational development.

WHEN SHOULD A UNIT PLAN BE ORGANIZED AND TAUGHT?

Each unit plan should be completely organized before any teaching begins. After some initial teaching on the basis of individual lesson plans, student teachers should be assigned a topic to prepare on a unit basis. The college supervisor should check and may assist in developing the unit plan during the first school visit.

HOW LONG SHOULD A UNIT BE?

The length of a unit depends on several factors: availability of materials, age of the students, curriculum guidelines, the class's level of interest, and the teacher's knowledge. In general, you would not want to design a new unit plan every week. On the other hand, if you stay with the same topic too long, students and teacher will get tired of it. Units can vary in length from a week or so to 4-6 weeks.

HOW IS A UNIT PLAN ORGANIZED?

Each unit plan should contain at least four major elements:

- The concept map.
- Overall goals or objectives for the entire unit.
- Specific objectives with related methods, procedures, or student activities.
- Evaluation.

Depending on the topic or subject, the maturity level, grade, or ability of the students, and the teacher's preferences, the plan could be fleshed out by adding such things as the sequence of topics or number of lessons needed to teach each subsection of the unit, or the materials required.

The Concept Map

A concept map is a diagram which organizes the content of a unit visually, providing, on one page, the outline of all information to be taught in the unit. (See Figures 6.1 and 6.2 for examples of concept maps.) Figure 6.1 shows the relationships between broader, more abstract concepts (shown in capital letters) and more concrete or specific concepts. The box at the top of the map shows where the unit begins, and the arrows indicate the path for working through the unit. The time allotment for parts of the unit can be identified on the map.

The process of drawing the concept map often helps a teacher conceptualize the content for the unit more clearly. It is also useful to look back at the map from time to time to make sure all the critical material has been covered. You may not agree with the particular concepts identified in Figures 6.1 and 6.2, but the important point is that the concept map be meaningful to the person who made it and must teach the unit.

Overall Goals or Objectives for the Unit

Look at your unit topic and the concept map you have constructed. Ask yourself "What are the most important things I want students to learn from this unit?"

FIGURE 6.1
CONCEPT MAP OF AN ENGLISH UNIT ON IDENTITY

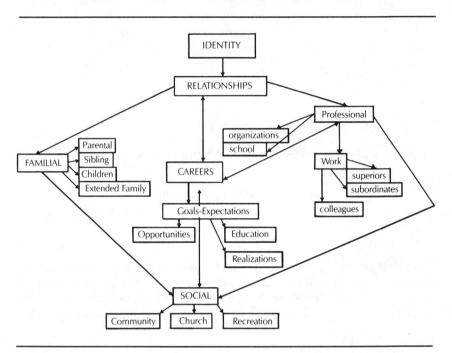

FIGURE 6.2
CONCEPT MAP FOR ALGEBRA AND REAL NUMBERS UNIT

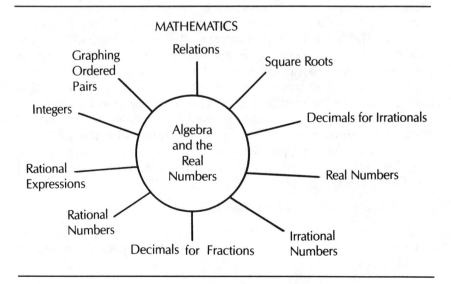

Consider your unit objectives in terms of the three major areas of educational growth: knowledge, skills, and values. Try to include each of these areas during the teaching of your unit.

It is not necessary to always have a long list of objectives. Decide which are most important. Use as few words as possible and write directly to the point. Behavioural or performance objectives are detailed and specific and are not usually appropriate for identifying the overall goals or objectives of an entire unit.

The following are examples of unit objectives written for various subjects in different grades. Although there is some individual variation in the style of writing goals and objectives, they all identify the main things that students are to learn during the unit.

OBJECTIVES FOR MATHEMATICS UNIT ON EXPONENTS AND LOGARITHMS

A. Knowledge

1. Any integer can be used as an exponent of any base.
2. Using powers with rational exponents, you can write radical expressions in exponential form.
3. The inverse of a relation is the relation obtained by interchanging the co-ordinates in each ordered pair in the given relation.
4. Given the graph of an exponential function, you can use it to find an approximation of any power of the base.
5. You obtain common logarithms of integral powers of 10 by writing the power in exponential form and noting the exponent.

B. Skills

1. Ability to graphically solve and estimate from given equations.
2. Ability to find logarithms by using a table.
3. Ability to solve equations using logarithms.

C. Values

1. Math can be fun.
2. Much of the way the physical world operates is based on mathematical principles.

MUSIC OBJECTIVES

A. Knowledge

1. To help the children learn about music by making music.
2. To learn that rhythm is found in many different forms.
3. To learn and be able to draw the eighth note, quarter note, and whole note.
4. To learn the concept of rhythm through listening, singing, playing, and moving.
5. To realize that music is all around us in our everyday lives.

B. Skills

1. To help the children experience and participate in music through creative play.
2. To help the children develop ways to communicate their own musical ideas to others.
3. To help the children develop musical skills in responding to rhythm, performing, listening, and creating.

C. Values

1. Music is for everyone's enjoyment.

SOCIAL STUDIES/GUIDANCE OBJECTIVES

A. Knowledge

1. Drugs and drug abuse have a negative effect on the lives of the user and the user's family and friends.
2. The relationship between parents and children can become tense and difficult as children begin to mature and form their own attitudes and identities.
3. As a person gets older, the boy/girl relationship often takes precedence over same-sex friendships.
4. Peer pressure is very difficult for adolescents to handle, and it often influences them to do things they may not want to.
5. As a person gets older and becomes aware of different ideas, it becomes increasingly difficult to decide what is wrong and what is right.

B. Skills

1. Group work.
2. Research skills: using an index and writing rough notes.

C. Values

1. Should parents criticize a teenager if the teenager's appearance and ideas do not conform to what the parents think is "normal"?
2. Should a person inform the police of a friend's illegal activities?
3. Should drug dealers always get the severest punishment available?
4. Should a young person be allowed to experiment with drugs to see what they are like?
5. Should a young person do certain things in order to be accepted by his or her peer group?

Specific Objectives, Procedures, and Student Activities

This is the major portion of your unit plan and will probably require several pages, depending on the size and length of the unit. This section may be organized in one of two formats: a page-by-page outline, or columns.

The following is an example of the outline format.

OBJECTIVE

Effective writing begins with high-interest, eye-catching statements.

PROCEDURES AND STUDENT ACTIVITIES

1. Read two examples of effective openings:
   — Mulroney speech, 1989.
   — *Star Phoenix* newspaper column.
2. Ask "What did the writer do to generate interest?"
3. With students' help, develop a list of effective openings.
4. Read two more examples of effective openings:
   — Editorial on disarmament.
   — Article: "Principles of Fuel-Injected Carburetors."
5. Ask "Which techniques did these authors use?"
6. Ask students to write an effective opening for "Fire Drill at School."
7. Have some students read their openings.
8. Give handouts on situations. Have students write "effective openings" for each situation, then hand them in for marking.

Examples of the column format are shown in Figures 6.3 and 6.4.

FIGURE 6.3
MULTIPLE-COLUMN UNIT-PLAN FORMAT

OBJECTIVES	CONCEPTS	CONTENT OUTLINE	MATERIALS	STRATEGIES/ PROCEDURES

FIGURE 6.4
TWO-COLUMN UNIT-PLAN FORMAT

Objective	Procedures/Student Activities
Effective writing begins with high-interest, eye-catching statements.	1. Read two examples of effective openings: — Mulroney speech, 1989. — *Star Phoenix* newspaper column. 2. Ask "What did the writer do to generate interest?" 3. With students' help, develop a list of effective openings. 4. Read two more examples of effective openings: — Editorial on disarmament. — Article: "Principles of Fuel-Injected Carburetors." 5. Ask "Which techniques did these authors use?" 6. Ask students to write an effective opening for "Fire Drill at School." 7. Have some students read their openings. 8. Give handouts on situations. Have students write "effective openings" for each situation, then hand them in for marking.

The column format has three major advantages: It presents a clearer overview of your unit; it helps you avoid getting bogged down in too many details, but provides as many details as necessary in the student activities column; and it reminds you of the direct relationship between procedures and student activities and the teacher's objectives.

There must be at least two columns: one for objectives and one for procedures/student activities. (See Figure 6.4) Many teachers find these two columns sufficient; others prefer another column or two for items such as content outline or materials, as shown in Figure 6.3.

In the "Objectives" column, write learning objectives and concepts. Identify skills that will be emphasized. Values and feelings should be noted in this column as well.

Information in the "Student Activities" column should be listed in detail and in outline form. Try to include a variety of student activities during your unit. If you have a guest speaker, think of several questions you might ask him or her. If a field trip is planned, list pre-trip and follow-up activities for the classroom. If a class discussion is planned, list several questions to guide the discussion, and state exactly what you want your students to get out of the discussion. The more detail you provide in this column, the less work you will need to do immediately prior to actually teaching the lesson, to the point where you are able to draw directly from your unit plan to fill in your day book and teach your lesson.

> **The examples in this book illustrate suggested planning techniques, but are not intended to represent the *only* way to plan lessons**

Figures 6.5, 6.6, and 6.7 provide examples of unit plans in different subjects and grade levels.

FIGURE 6.5
PLAN FOR HEALTH UNIT ON ORGANS OF THE BODY

Objectives	Activities	Materials
I. Introduce organs of the body and research one organ.	1. Introduction (motivational set) — look at pp. 36, 37, 38 in *You and Your Health*. Discuss the pictures and questions. 2. List six organs of the body (heart, skin, stomach, lungs, brain, skeleton). 3. Refer students to the resource books displayed in the room. 4. Students must tell four interesting things about one organ, draw a picture, and record the title, author, and publisher of the resource books used.	foolscap markers coloured paper stencils
II. Learn about the location, appearance and function of the brain.	1. Motivational set — a giant body frame is displayed on the bulletin board. Students cut out similar but smaller frames and paste them in their notebooks. 2. Discuss the brain. Individuals who wrote reports on the brain share the information they found.	body frame (small) body frame (large) brain (small) brain (large) handout — "The Brain"

FIGURE 6.6
PLAN FOR SCIENCE UNIT ON SOUND

Objectives	Activities
Our world is full of sounds, and sounds are very important to us.	Class Discussion (Guide Questions) 1. What do you do when you hear a fire-truck siren? 2. How do you feel? 3. What other sounds might you hear at a basketball game or other sports event? 4. Do any sounds stand out, or is the sound just one big jumble of noise? 5. Can you think of any sounds that occur at certain times of the day?
Sounds help us know what is happening around us. Sounds are made by vibrating objects. Sounds are high or low, loud or soft.	1. Introduce new word: *vibrate* ("moving to and fro"). 2. Read "Listen!" (p. 212). Have students make a list of all the sounds they hear in one minute. 3. Let the class experiment with what happens when they snap the ruler gently and then with more force (p. 212). 4. Have the students identify which vibrating objects make sounds that can be heard, and which do not (p. 213, "Vibrations and Sound"). 5. Discuss question 4 in the text.

FIGURE 6.7
PLAN FOR ENGLISH UNIT ON A NOVEL

Objectives	Content Outline	Student Activities
Bryon and Mark have a special relationship and are like brothers, although they are not actually related.	1. Description of Bryon's neighbourhood. 2. Introduction of main characters in novel — Mark and Bryon — as well as supporting characters — M&M and Charlie. 3. Relationship between Bryon and Mark.	1. Read Chapter 1 of novel aloud in class. 2. Answer questions from handout: a) What kind of neighbourhood do Bryon and Mark live in? Provide evidence to support your answer. b) Describe Mark's physical and character traits. c) Who is M&M? What is he like? d) Who is Charlie? e) What kind of person is Bryon? f) What kind of relationship do Bryon and Mark have? 3. Correct the questions in class.
A person is not always rewarded or commended when he/she does something that he/she considers right. (Main understanding.)	1. Bryon and authority. 2. Incident between Mick Chambers and Connie.	1. Read Chapter 2 aloud in class. 2. Answer questions from handout: a) Why doesn't Bryon accept authority? b) What sort of boy is Mike Chambers? c) After what Mike did, why did Connie tell her friends "Kill the white man"? 3. Correct the questions in class.

The following is a checklist of some teaching methods which might be incorporated into your unit. Most of them will need to be amplified in your "Student Activities" column.

Class discussion
Students contribute to note-
   making
Asking questions
Making time-lines
Map work
Developing chalkboard notes
Inquiry — drawing inferences
Group work — making
   conclusions
Field trips
Role-playing
Simulation games
Concept teaching
Answering and discussing
   questionnaires
Guest speaker
Reading for the main idea
Guided reading
Oral reports
Writing a report
Writing an editorial
Analyzing a cartoon
Controlled research
Prioritizing value concepts in
   given situations

Word-choice exercises
Values continuum
Valuing/decision-making
Analyzing an issue
Comparing contradictory evidence
Conducting a survey
   (questionnaire)
Interviews — oral history
Self-instructional learning stations
Games of clue
Writing personal position papers
Writing position papers from
   another's perspective
Writing historical or cultural
   newspaper
Symbols
Crossword puzzles
Word scrambles
Developing a chart
Classifying and categorizing
Group reports — written, oral
Belief statements

It is helpful to distinguish "methods" and "student activities" listed above from "materials." Several of the above methods and activities might be used with various materials. Example of materials on which methods or activities could be based include:

Textbooks
Reference books
Photographs and slides
Filmstrips
Audio-filmstrip kit
Records
Audio tapes
Diaries
Reports
Newspapers

Pamphlets
Graphs
Artifacts and objects
Kinship charts
Sociograms
Data/Retrieval charts
Map jigsaw puzzles
Position papers
Government documents
Archival records

Magazines	Biographies and autobiographies
Fact sheets	Government reports
Questionnaires and surveys	Descriptive paragraphs/statements
Question sheets	written by the teacher
Statistics	Quotes
Poems	Maps and globes
Cartoons	Almanacs
Encyclopedias	Computer software

Finally, describe how you would "wrap up" your unit. What would the culminating activity be — a field trip, guest speaker, special display or performance, game, special film? Try to think of one activity which would pull the whole unit together.

Closing does *not* include a review or a final test. Those are part of the next section — evaluation.

Evaluation

Evaluation is part of the educational process in all school subject areas. Good teachers have a philosophy about evaluation as well as a knowledge of various techniques of evaluation. Evaluation provides feedback to students and their teacher on the effectiveness of the teacher's teaching as well as on the students' learning. It is a guide for change, revision, remediation, and progress.

The teaching process becomes a coherent whole when there is consistency among objectives, teaching methods, student activities, and evaluations.

There are five principles for evaluating a unit. Evaluation involves collecting and judging information. The following principles should be followed:

1. Evaluation should be related to the objectives.
2. Evaluation should employ a variety of techniques in collecting information.
3. Evaluation should consider knowledge, skills, and values.
4. Evaluation should assess students beyond Level I in the area of knowledge.
5. Evaluation should be both formative and summative in nature.

Tell students about assignments at the outset of the unit.

List your directions in writing, either on a handout or on the chalkboard. Tell students your expectations for each part of the assignment, as well as the form or style in which you want it handed in. Specific guidelines help students complete assignments successfully.

The following is an example of an evaluation component in a unit plan.

Assignment	Value	Due Date
Weekly Assignments	20%	Oct. 3-24
Learning Centre Contract	10%	Oct. 10
Co-operative Group Work	10%	Oct. 15
Co-operative Individual Work	10%	Oct. 15
Oral Presentation	10%	Oct. 20
Open-Ended Story	10%	Oct. 24
Final Exam	30%	Oct. 28
	100%	

Chapter 12 deals with evaluation in more detail.

WHAT IS THE RELATIONSHIP BETWEEN LESSON PLANS, UNIT PLANS AND THE DAY-PLAN BOOK?

Once a unit plan has been developed, there should no longer be a need to write individual lesson plans. The unit should be planned in sufficient detail to enable the teacher to draw from it to teach individual lessons. However, a few specific notes remain to be included in the teacher's day-plan book.

DAY PLANS

Experienced teachers do not write out detailed lesson plans, but keep a day plan in which to write notes about what they will do in each class period.

Figure 6.8 shows a page from a day-plan book made by an elementary teacher; Figure 6.9, one made by a secondary teacher.

Day-plan books are usually required by the school administration. They serve two purposes: (1) They are essential in order for a teacher to be organized for each class period, and (2) they show a substitute teacher what to do on that day if the regular teacher is unable to come to school.

FIGURE 6.8
ELEMENTARY DAY PLAN

Monday

9:00-9:10	Opening Exercises/Announcements/Current Events
9:10-9:20	Show and Tell
9:20-10:30	*Reading*: Group A — Read the story Group B — Workbooks pp. 18, 19 Group C — Oral Reading
10:30-10:45	RECESS
10:45-11:30	*Arithmetic*: Groups put exercises on the board. Review "borrowing" concept in subtraction. Do p. 19.
11:30-12:00	*Health/Guidance*: Analyze breakfast on basis of the food chart. *Spelling*:
12:00-1:00	NOON
1:00-1:40	*Social Studies*: Oral questions on the pictures. Develop a summary chart on the board.
1:40-2:15	*Language*: Develop sentences using concepts from Social Studies. Note capital letters and periods.
2:15-2:30	RECESS
2:30-3:00	*Science*: Demonstrate jet propulsion using a balloon. Write up the experiment. *Art*:
3:00-3:30	*Music*: *Phys Ed*: Demonstrate foot and arm motion in throwing. Play dodge ball.

FIGURE 6.9
SECONDARY DAY PLAN

Monday, Day 4

09:00-09:05	Announcements; movement to classes.
09:05-09:35	*English 10.* Topic: Story — "The Way Up," p. 184. Objective: Financial success can have negative side effects. Vocabulary development. Read and discuss the theme.
09:35-09:40	Break.
09:40-10:20	*Physics 30.* Topic: Gravity. Objective: Earth's gravity causes tidal pull. Develop diagram on p. 179. Finish for homework.
10:20-10:25	Break.
10:25-11:15	*Phys Ed 11.* Topic: Tumbling — forward roll. Objective: Motion dissipates energy. Demonstrate the roll. Practise in pairs.
11:15-11:20	Break.
11:20-12:00	*English 30.* Topic: Essay writing. Objective: An essay has distinctive sections. Give directions. Limit the topic to write on. Emphasize the introduction. Note a personal view in the summary. Finish for homework.
12:00-13:00	NOON HOUR.
13:00-13:40	*Home Room — English 20.* Topic: Vocabulary development. Objective: Adjectives are describing words. Brainstorm from p. 48. Homework: exercises on p. 52.
13:40-13:45	Break.
13:45-14:35	*English 10.* Topic: Story — "The Way Up." Objective: Stories have morals for daily living. Write alternative endings to the story. Ending must have a moral message. Finish for homework.
14:35-14:40	Break.
14:40-15:30	*Phys Ed 9.* Topic: Soccer — passing. Objective: (1) Turn foot to side-kick passes. (2) Lead the receiver with your pass. Demonstrate. Practise in pairs, progressively increasing the distance. Scrimmage game near the end.

The best time to fill in your day-plan book for the next day's lessons is as soon as possible after the end of each class period. Sometimes this can be done while the students put away their books from this class and take out the ones for the next period, or while they exchange rooms between classes. Some teachers do it during recess or a study hall period, or before going for lunch. The sooner you fill out next period's activities, the easier it is to remember exactly where you want to begin and what you want to do in the next class. Teaching a full load of classes requires keeping your day-plan book up to date.

Weekly Timetable

In high schools and in some middle-years grades, the school administration takes responsibility for making the weekly timetable.

The curriculum guide or Ministry of Education regulations specify the approximate time to be spent on each subject.

Year Plan

A year or semester plan helps teachers ensure that they allow enough time to teach required topics and also fit in special projects or events. It also helps teachers avoid being in the middle of a unit of work when the Christmas and Easter breaks occurs.

Figures 6.10, 6.11, and 6.12 are examples of year plans.

Figure 6.10
English Semester Plan of Five Units Organized by Literary Forms

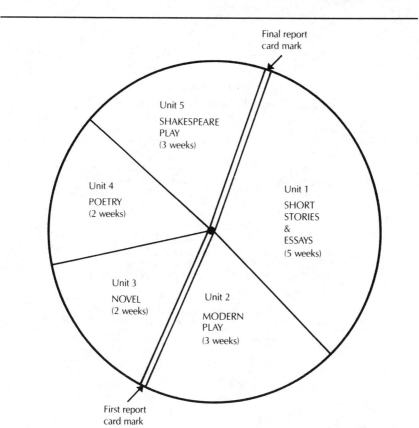

FIGURE 6.11
AN ELEMENTARY-SCHOOL YEAR PLAN

	Themes for the Year
September:	Harvest, Fall Equinox, Spring in Australia, Grandparents' Day, Rosh Hashanah (Jewish New Year)
October:	Thanksgiving Day (Canada), Hallowe'en, United Nations Day, Citizens' Day, Columbus Day (U.S.A.)
November:	Remembrance Day (Canada), Veterans Day (U.S.A.), Louis Riel Day, Thanksgiving Day (U.S.A.)
December:	Christmas, Winter Solstice, Hanukkah, Human Rights Day
January:	Winter, the new year, review of last year's current events
February:	Groundhog Day, Valentine's Day, Ash Wednesday
March:	St. Patrick's Day, Spring Equinox
April:	Easter, Palm Sunday, Passover, Spring
May:	Spring, Mother's Day, Victoria Day (Canada), Memorial Day (U.S.A.)
June:	Father's Day, Summer Solstice

FIGURE 6.12
AN ELEMENTARY-SCHOOL SCIENCE YEAR PLAN

Date	Unit	Topic/Theme
Sept. 4-15	1	Observing Things
Sept. 15-Nov. 30	2	Animals and Adaptation
Dec. 1-15	3	Plants and Adaptation
Dec. 15-20		Christmas Activities
	Christmas Break	
January	4	Weather
Feb. 1-15	5	Exploring Ocean Depths
Feb. 15-Mar. 15	6	Exploring Matter
Mar. 15-Apr. 19	7	Electricity and Magnetism
	Easter Break	
Apr. 20-May 15	8	Understanding Matter
May 15-June	9	Machines Around Us

Part III:
APPROACHES TO INSTRUCTION

Chapter Seven:
TEACHER-DIRECTED INSTRUCTION

Main Understandings

In this chapter you will learn the following:

1. The effectiveness of a teaching approach depends on whether structured or flexible content is being taught.
2. Systematic instruction is effective in teaching structured content and increasing students' academic achievement.
3. Good teachers are capable of using different teaching methods for both structured and flexible content.

Choosing a Teaching Method

Figure 7.1 leads the teacher through the decision-making process to arrive at the most appropriate method for teaching in a given situation. First, the teacher considers factors affecting the choice of teaching method: the backgrounds of students (their age, maturity, interests, experiences, and intelligence), availability of materials, the nature of the particular topic or subject, the intent of your lesson (*e.g.*, to explore or enhance attitudes, to teach basic principles, to present new alternatives), the amount of time available, and the teacher's own background and experience.

83

FIGURE 7.1

CHOOSING A TEACHING METHOD

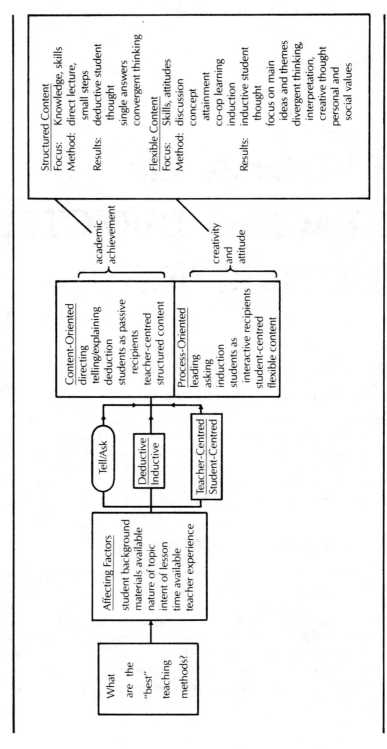

Using this information, the teacher then decides whether the instruction will be teacher-centred or student-centred. Will the teacher *tell* or *ask* in order to convey the information? Will the approach be *inductive* or *deductive*? The teacher must then ask "Will I emphasize content or process?" Finally, after weighing creative and attitudinal outcomes against academic outcomes, the teacher selects either structure or flexible content.

This chapter will focus on teaching structured content through systematic instruction, but first we will contrast this approach with other approaches suited to flexible content.

DEDUCTIVE AND INDUCTIVE TEACHING

In deductive teaching, the teacher begins with a generalization and then offers specific evidence, details, facts, and examples to support the general principle. For example, a teacher could begin a lesson by stating that an increase in bank lending rates can lower inflation. Students would then be given examples of how this principle operates.

Inductive teaching begins with specific examples and leads toward a generalization or main principle. In the example above, a teacher using an inductive approach would offer the class several examples of higher bank rates and prices of various goods. Eventually, the teacher would ask "How do these higher interest rates affect the rate of inflation?" Students would use the specific examples to arrive at a general conclusion that higher lending rates can lower inflation.

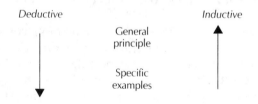

TEACHER-CENTRED AND STUDENT-CENTRED TEACHING

In the teacher-centred approach, the teacher is the centre of attention, directing, demonstrating, and orchestrating the class from the front of the room. Students tend to absorb information passively.

In the student-centred approach, the focus is on the student as an active learner. Class discussion, student-to-student interaction, group work, and project work characterize student-centred teaching.

CONTENT ORIENTATION AND PROCESS ORIENTATION

The characteristics of content-oriented and process-oriented teaching are contrasted in Figure 7.1. However, the two approaches are not mutually exclusive. For example, content-oriented teachers sometimes ask questions during their classes, and process-oriented teachers sometimes explain things to their students.

Neither general approach to teaching is necessarily superior to the other. Either approach can be used effectively or ineffectively, and the choice of approach should depend on the purpose of your instruction. There is research evidence, for example, to suggest that academic achievement is enhanced when content-oriented teaching methods are used effectively. Other research findings suggest that a process-oriented approach may be more effective in enhancing creativity and attitude. Of course, even these two statements are subject to exception and interpretation.

Both approaches can be suited to elementary or high-school students, and to bright students or students with less academic ability, in the appropriate situation.

STRUCTURED CONTENT AND FLEXIBLE CONTENT

The effectiveness of an approach to teaching depends on numerous factors, one of which is the content we are teaching. As shown in Figure 7.2, structured content focuses on the basic knowledge and skills of the subject, while flexible content focuses on creativity, interpretation, and attitude.

Beginning teachers tend to focus on structured content. As they acquire experience and confidence, they pay more attention to developing flexible content. Teachers must be able to deal with both kinds of content. Some subjects, such as Mathematics or Physical Education, may lend themselves more to structured content, whereas others, such as Art or Literature, may lend themselves more to flexible content.

Criticism has been levelled at teaching styles associated with each kind of content. For example, it has been said that students find structured-content classes boring. But in fact success in learning motivates students to work harder and learn more. Lack of success is discouraging and results in negative attitudes. Effective teachers do not present facts in isolation; they use them to lead students toward understanding key concepts and ideas. Although structured content has been associated with "telling" and "lecturing," effective teachers also use questions to help guide students' learning.

FIGURE 7.2
STRUCTURED CONTENT AND FLEXIBLE CONTENT

Structured Content	Flexible Content
Subject Matter	
Math; grammar and vocabulary (in English and other languages); musical notations; factual components of social studies and science	English composition; creative writing; analysis of literature; interpretation of stories and social issues; problem-solving; fluency in conversation; reading comprehension; evaluation of ideas; appreciation; exploration of students' interests, feelings, attitudes, and values
Methodology	
Teacher demonstrations, lectures	Encouraging student choice and participation
Teacher-centred "stand-up" teaching	Student-centred group "indirect" teaching
Tendency toward deductive thought by students	Tendency toward inductive thought by students
Step-by-step explicit instruction	Step-by-step instruction is not necessary or desirable
Teaching toward single answer, convergent thinking	Focus on main ideas and themes, creative thought
	Teaching toward interpretive responses and divergent thinking

Conversely, some critics claim that flexible-content teaching methods fail to teach students sufficient information. But effective teachers provide enough information to enable students to make sound judgments.

Both kinds of content and corresponding approaches to teaching can occur within a single lesson. For example, the early part of a lesson or unit in Social Studies can contain highly structured content such as the components and relationships of the bodies within the United Nations. Then the teacher may switch to flexible content, asking students to analyze various operations performed by the U.N. and its suborganizations.

APPROACHES TO INSTRUCTION

Various approaches can be taken to teach structured or flexible content. For structured content, teacher-directed instruction (the subject of the rest of this chapter) and conceptual teaching (to be discussed in Chapter 8) are often appropriate. For flexible content, approaches such as inquiry/discovery and co-operative learning may work better. These approaches will be discussed in Chapter 9.

Teacher-Directed Instruction

Rosenshine and Stevens (1986) reviewed numerous studies which supported the principle that a specific set of teaching procedures results in increased student cognitive achievement in learning structured content. This approach has been called "systematic instruction," "effective instruction," or "direct instruction." In this book, we refer to it as teacher-directed instruction. Outlines for two variations on a teacher-directed instruction plan follow.

LESSON FORMAT 1

1. *Review Previous and Related Work*
   The teacher can remind students about the previous day's work, reviewing main concepts, conclusions, and/or skills. A more effective approach is to ask the students to answer review questions. A third approach is to take up the previous day's homework assignment. Reteaching can be done if necessary, but the review should be brief and direct.

2. *Introduce the Lesson*
   Two things should occur in the introduction. First, the teacher must give the students an overview of the lesson topic and identify the key point they are to learn. If the lesson's learning objective is to be developed during the lesson and arrived at by students at the end of the lesson, use the introduction to tell students what they will be doing in the lesson.

   A second thing which must occur is motivation. How can you get the class interested in learning more about the lesson's topic? Try telling a brief story, reading a quote, providing a brief demonstration, or asking a question to arouse students' curiosity.

   The beginning of a lesson may not necessarily follow the order presented above (review, overview, motivation). In some cases, it will be better to provide the overview first, then conduct a brief review, and finally provide some motivation before presenting the main body of your lesson. Whichever order you choose, these three parts of a lesson should require only a short time to present.

3. *Present the Information*
   Proceed with step-by-step instruction, providing explicit explanations and emphasizing key points.

   Ask questions to ensure that students understand each point. Summarize main points, or ask students to summarize in their own words. Reteach if students are having difficulty. Continue to highlight each main point and try to stay on schedule. Provide instructions, illustrations, examples, and models in your demonstration. Keep asking the class questions until student responses are at least 80 percent accurate, even if some repetition and reteaching are required.

4. *Guided and Independent Practice*
Usually practice occurs in seatwork or at individual stations in the lab or on the gym floor. Offer closer guidance and supervision at first. Spend time with each student, correcting errors and reteaching as necessary. More effective teachers spend a greater amount of time on guided practice than do less effective ones. They devote more time to asking questions, correcting errors, repeating new material, and solving problems under teacher guidance. Students are given sufficient time to practise their new skills and apply new knowledge in a controlled environment in which they can get immediate feedback.

FIGURE 7.3

CHECKLIST FOR PLANNING A TEACHER-DIRECTED LESSON

1. Review
   - tell
   - ask questions
   - focus on key points
   - check homework

2. Introduction/Overview
   - tell the topic
   - tell what the lesson is about
   - tell main learning principle
   - tell what students will do
   - motivate

3. Present the Information
   - small steps
   - check periodically for understanding
   - ask questions
   - summarize main points
   - tell students
   - review questions
   - reteach if necessary
   - maintain rapid pace
   - aim for high accuracy in student responses

4. Guided and Independent Practice
   - provide close guidance initially
   - rotate among students
   - give positive feedback
   - correct errors
   - reteach
   - aim for high accuracy in student responses

Independent practice may occur in follow-up seatwork, individualized practice within a class period, homework, or periodic reviews and tests. Avoid assigning homework if students have not had previous success with the work.

The above steps are summarized in Figure 7.3.

LESSON FORMAT 2

1. *Motivational Set*
   The teacher attracts interest or attention at the beginning of a lesson, ties in the scope and sequence of the lesson with other lessons and/ or reviews, and relates it to past and future topics or ideas.

2. *Stating Objectives*
   At the outset of a lesson, tell students what they will be doing, or identify the topic for study (*e.g.,* "Today we are going to learn about . . ."). The teacher often may not want to tell students the learning objective of the lesson, preferring instead to lead students toward discovering this objective as the lesson progresses. At this point in the lesson, the objective would be identified only in terms of student activities rather than in terms of learning principles.

3. *Activities*
   These must relate to the lesson's objectives.

4. *Sequence/Time Frame*
   The lesson should follow a definite sequence that can be marked off in time intervals. For example:

Minutes	Events in the Lesson
1-2	Motivational set.
1	Explain the objective in terms of what students will be doing.
10-15	Give directions. Demonstrate.
20	Seatwork or other class follow-up activities.
5	Summary and review. Prepare to change classes.

5. *Transitions*
   The teacher should move smoothly and swiftly from one activity or one point in the lesson to the next. Don't let students waste time when moving into groups or from their desks to tables.

6. *Stressing Objectives and Difficult Points*
   If the teacher can anticipate students' problems, she or he can emphasize important aspects of the topic and clarify directions in advance.

7. *Summarizing and Concluding*
   The teacher either reviews the material in the lesson or, better yet, asks students to respond to several important review questions.

8. *Practice*
   The teacher gives students an opportunity to practise what they have learned.

Although all eight components are assessed in evaluating a teacher's performance, common sense recognizes that it is not always appropriate to have every step in every kind of lesson every day. These steps do become important when new and difficult material is presented in a class.

Two other forms of teacher-directed instruction are the interactive lecture and the demonstration lesson. They are outlined below.

THE INTERACTIVE LECTURE OR TEACHER-LED DISCUSSION

Teachers do a great deal of "telling." This provides opportunities for active participation through asking questions which students can answer briefly. It offers students an opportunity to paraphrase, practise, discuss, or derive implications from the information.

Thought-provoking questions are asked. The teacher projects meaningful and interesting aspects of the topic, and personalizes the presentation by relating the topic to the experiences of students. Key points are emphasized through pause, repetition, query, humour, and summary of the presentation. Finally, students are required to organize the information in a meaningful way.

The list that follows indicates the main points to consider when *planning* an interactive lecture or discussion.

- Clearly state the purpose and major theme.
- Sequence the main points and subpoints.
- Limit the scope of the topic.
- Set a time limit. Keep the lecture as short as possible.

(Tell them what you're going to tell them.)

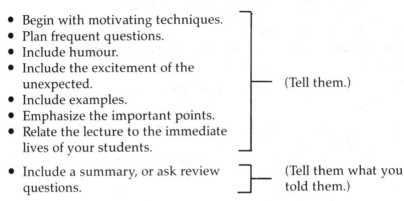

- Begin with motivating techniques.
- Plan frequent questions.
- Include humour.
- Include the excitement of the unexpected.
- Include examples.
- Emphasize the important points.
- Relate the lecture to the immediate lives of your students.

(Tell them.)

- Include a summary, or ask review questions.

(Tell them what you told them.)

The following points should be kept in mind while *delivering* an interactive lecture.

- Observe students to detect restlessness, confusion, or boredom.
- Use a strong and clear voice.
- Modulate your tone of voice.
- Use clear, simple, and concise language.
- Employ appropriate gestures.
- Stay on the topic.
- Ask frequent questions.
- Encourage a spirit of inquiry and thought.

THE DEMONSTRATION

Showing students how something operates or how it is done is a direct teaching approach. The following list will help you plan an effective demonstration lesson.

- Introduction
  - describe the procedure
  - define the purpose
  - describe merits and warnings/cautions
- Verbal description during the demonstration.
- Ensure that everyone can see the demonstration clearly.
- Proceed at a slow and steady pace.
- Demonstrate the entire process first, then break it down into parts and demonstrate each part separately (the whole/part method).
- Repeat demonstrations when necessary.
- Walk students through the process under close supervision.

A demonstration is usually accompanied by follow-up drill and practice. This follow-up helps keep students motivated by informing them of their progress. Students can practise individually with close supervision from the teacher. In follow-up drills, the teacher should:

- Tell students why the drill is needed.
- Communicate a goal and standards of excellence.
- Keep drills short and maintain a brisk pace.
- Allow students to contribute to planning and evaluating the practice sessions.

Think of a unit of study you might teach. Would an interactive lecture be your best instructional approach for introducing the unit, teaching content, or making use of your special training and experience in a particular area?

Are there school, community or student resources available for demonstrations? Who would do them — you or your students?

Chapter Eight:
CONCEPTUAL
TEACHING

Main Understandings

In this chapter you will learn the following:

1. Facts, concepts, and main understandings are interrelated components of knowledge.
2. The basic model for teaching a concept involves critical attributes, examples, and non-examples.

The Structure of Knowledge

Knowledge, regardless of the topic or subject, has a structure based on facts, concepts, and main understandings. The ultimate goal of teaching should not be to make students memorize facts, but to lead them toward an understanding of principles and key ideas. The accumulation of data is, however, necessary to the development of major ideas (concepts) and conclusions or understandings (generalizations).

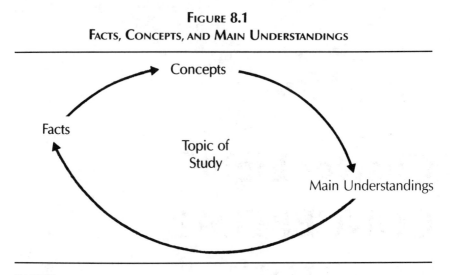

FIGURE 8.1
FACTS, CONCEPTS, AND MAIN UNDERSTANDINGS

FACTS

Facts are the individual building blocks of knowledge, but each isolated fact is relatively unimportant. *It is only when facts support and relate to one another that they become valuable in building knowledge.* Good teachers have learned to select only facts which lead toward the understanding of ideas they are trying to teach.

A fact is a specific or detailed piece of information supported by all the available evidence. With new evidence, a fact might change. For example, at one time students in Social Studies were taught that Christopher Columbus was the first European to "discover" the New World. New evidence has shown that the Vikings had sailed to the New World and formed settlements prior to the voyages of Columbus.

An Example of Facts, Concepts, and a Main Understanding

Facts: There was 8 cm of rainfall last summer. There was 12 cm of snowfall last winter.

Concepts: precipitation, seasons.

Main Understanding: The amount of precipitation varies from season to season.

CONCEPTS

Concepts are main ideas or sets of ideas that can be described in a single word or a few words. We teach concepts every day and with every topic.

"Symbolism" is a concept. "Linear progression" is a concept. "Fission" and "fusion" are concepts. "Full-court press," "kinship," and "threshold" are concepts. Every topic and subject consists of many concepts.

If you were teaching the concept of "urbanization," there would be several related concepts that you might want your students to understand. You might focus on the concept of "hinterland" and the various natural and human resources in a city's hinterland. Investigation of the value of goods, and of transportation networks related to the city and its hinterland, could provide information that would help students grasp the broader concept of urbanization.

Concepts range from concrete to abstract. A concrete concept is one which may be readily seen or touched by students. For example, you could bring into the classroom an ancient Indian stone hammer. Students could examine it. They could pick it up as you discuss the concept of a hammer and its uses, how it was made, where it was found, its age, etc. Other concepts are more abstract. You cannot touch or pick up a concept such as "poetic justice" or "state of equilibrium." In many ways, teaching consists of making abstract concepts more concrete for students by designing experiences or providing examples.

Some concepts are specific, such as "telephone" or "integer"; others are more encompassing, such as "communication" or "algebra."

MAIN UNDERSTANDINGS

Main understandings are statements which show the relationship between two or more concepts. They are written in sentence form. When all the available evidence supports the main understanding, it becomes a fact.

The learning objective for your lesson plan is a main understanding. Main understandings and concepts are the guideposts of learning, when supported by related and appropriate facts.

RELATING FACTS, CONCEPTS, AND MAIN UNDERSTANDINGS

Fact: (1) Usually a statement. (2) All available evidence supports it. (3) A piece of specific information — a detail.

Concept: (1) Usually a single word or two. (2) A category, idea, or set of ideas. (3) May be concrete or abstract.

Main understanding: (1) A statement in sentence form. (2) Shows the relationship between two or more concepts.

When all available evidence supports a main understanding, that main understanding then becomes a fact. (This circular pattern is illustrated in Figure 8.1.) A fact remains a fact only as long as all available evidence supports it. New evidence can change a fact.

Look at the following example of how facts are used to lead toward concepts, and concepts toward a main understanding.

An Example Relating Facts, Concepts, and Main Understandings

Facts: A dog has hair. A dog has four legs. A dog barks, growls, and snarls. A dog bites. A dog wags its tail to be friendly.

A cat meows and purrs. A cat climbs trees. A cat scratches. A cat hunts mice and birds. A cat twitches its tail when angry.

Concepts: Dog. Cat.

After teaching the concept of "dog," the teacher would then proceed to teach the next concept, "cat." When both concepts were taught, the teacher would then ask, "What could we say, in general, about cats and dogs?"

Main understanding: *Dogs* and *cats* are *tame animals.*

If available evidence supports this main understanding, then the main understanding will become a fact.

Note that in this main understanding a new concept has been introduced — tame animals. If students do not understand the main understanding, it may be necessary for the teacher to focus on the concept of tame animals before proceeding.

TEACHING A CONCEPT LESSON

The steps involved in a concept lesson are described below.

1. *Identify the Critical Attributes of the Concept*
   Critical attributes are the essential characteristics that must exist in order for it to be a concept. They may be viewed as facts supporting the concept.

2. *Provide Examples and/or Non-Examples*
   It is always necessary to provide at least one example of the concept. If the concept is abstract to your students or if it is a complicated concept, several examples will be necessary. With relatively simple concepts, it may not be necessary or appropriate to provide non-examples. Again, however, with more complicated concepts it will be necessary to show students both examples and non-examples of the concept. Examples may be presented in several ways — explained by the teacher, or found in a variety of sources such as pictures, books,

filmstrips, graphs, news reports, magazine articles or diaries. The textbook may provide examples as well.

3. *Discriminate Between Examples and Non-Examples*
The examples and non-examples used in this step should be similar to those in the previous step, but not exactly the same.

The following example illustrates the use of the first three streps in teaching a concept. We will call this concept a "zork."

This is a zork. (Example.)

This is not a zork. (Non-example.)

This is a zork.

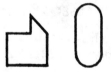

These are not zorks.

This is a zork.

What is a zork? What are its critical attributes?

A zork must have the critical attributes of (1) a straight line, and (2) a curved line. This is an example of a *definition* of a concept.

Can you discriminate between zorks and non-zorks in the figures below?

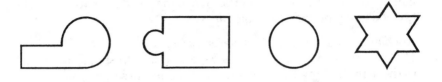

The first two figures are zorks; the last two figures are not. If you can tell zorks from non-zorks and identify their critical attributes, the teacher could assume you now understand the concept of "zork."

In the example, the teacher gave examples and non-examples of the concept first, then asked students to identify the critical attributes. This sequence is call indirect instruction. The teacher could also have used direct instruction, in which the critical attributes are defined for students first, then examples and non-examples are presented.

Which sequence is better? It depends on the concept you are teaching, the students, and the way in which you decide to organize the teaching of the concept.

4. *Provide Implications and Applications of the Concept*
   What does the concept mean?
   To which situations would it apply?

5. *Express Feelings About the Concept*
   Once students have learned the concept, there should be opportunities to express and assess their feelings about this concept. This provides opportunities to "internalize" (give meaning to) the concept.

EXAMPLE OF A CONCEPT LESSON: "ICING"

Let's look at a concept which is not usually taught in the classroom. Then you can apply these ideas to the teaching of a concept in a subject you might teach.

Consider the concept of "icing" in hockey. Icing occurs when the puck travels across the red line and goal line in the opponent's half of the rink. When icing occurs, the referee blows a whistle and the teams face off in the zone of the team guilty of icing the puck. Icing is based on the rule that teams are not permitted to shoot the puck the entire length of the ice.

To teach this concept, you might employ the following steps:

1. Identify the *critical attributes* of the concept.
   a) The puck travels across the centre red line and goal line.
   b) The puck must travel uninterrupted.
   c) The puck must cross the goal line somewhere between a goalpost and the side boards, without crossing the area of the goal crease.

d) Either each team has the same number of players on the ice, or the offending team has a larger number of players on the ice.

e) In the opinion of the referee, no player of the team in the defending zone is able to make a play for the puck.

2. Provide *examples*.

a) Team A cannot get the puck out of its own zone. Team B is about to score a goal. A Team A player shoots the puck down to the other end of the ice.

b) A Team A player carries the puck out of his own end. Before reaching the red line at centre, he passes to a teammate. His teammate misses the pass and the puck goes into the opposition end and hits the end boards.

3. Provide *non-examples*.

a) A Team A player shoots the puck slowly the length of the ice from his own end. A Team B player skates slowly after the puck, waiting for it to cross the goal line at the end of the rink before touching it. (Critical attribute (e) is missing.)

b) Team A got a penalty and is playing five against six. Team B is pressing to score a goal in Team A's end of the ice. In desperation, Team A shoots the puck the length of the ice. (Critical attribute (d) is missing.)

c) Team A shoots the puck the length of the ice. However, before the puck crosses the goal line, the Team B goalie skates out from the goal area, stops the puck, and quickly passes it to one of the Team B defencemen. (Critical attributes (a) and (b) are missing.)

It may be helpful, in some cases, to note any non-essential critical attributes of the concept. For example, the intention of the player is not a factor in determining an icing infraction. Whether the puck was shot the length of the ice intentionally or by accident has nothing to do with whether or not the referee calls the icing infraction.

4. *Discriminate* between examples and non-examples.
   Use examples and non-examples similar to those just mentioned, but vary the situations.

5. *Provide implications/applications* of the concept.

a) A penalized team playing with fewer players has the advantage of being permitted to shoot the puck away from its end of the ice.

b) A team guilty of icing the puck is penalized by having the puck faced off in its own end of the rink.

c) The icing rule discourages the long breakaway pass (which is permitted in basketball).

6. *Express feelings* about the concept.
   a) The icing rule is good because it gives a penalized team a better chance against stronger opponents.
   b) The icing rule is bad because it delays the game by stopping play more often.

ORGANIZING TOPICS FOR CONCEPTUAL TEACHING

Following are some examples of how a teacher could approach teaching various school subjects. These examples refer only to the first two parts of the concept teaching model — (1) identifying the critical attributes, and (2) providing examples and non-examples.

PHYSICS

Topic: Motion Along a Straight Line

In teaching about motion along a straight line, one major concept would be "displacement."
  The critical attributes are:
1. a straight line
2. position A on the line
3. position B on the line
4. movement of an object from point A to point B

At some point during the lesson, the teacher might include some facts about displacement:

1. If an object moves from A to B, the displacement is given by the difference, A - B.
2. Displacement may be negative or positive, depending only on the direction of the motion, not on which side of the origin point the movement has occurred.

In the diagram below, arrow 1 is an example of positive displacement. Arrow 2 is a non-example of positive displacement (*i.e.*, it is an example of negative displacement). Similarly, arrow 3 is an example of negative displacement because it indicates movement toward lower numbers on the scale. For this same reason, arrow 3 can also be regarded as a non-example of positive displacement. Based on this information, would arrow 4 be an example or a non-example of negative displacement?

The critical attribute for positive displacement is that movement is toward higher numbers on the scale, regardless of which side of zero the movement occurs on. The critical attribute for negative displacement is that movement is toward lower numbers on the scale, regardless of which side of zero the movement occurs on.

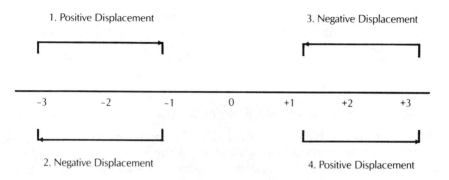

Other concepts relating to motion along a straight line need to be taught as well, including "constant velocity," "instantaneous velocity," "acceleration," and "constant acceleration." Examples and non-examples could be provided through graphs and problem situations such as breaking the sound barrier or firing a rocket from a spaceship.

These examples and non-examples would require students to consider the relationships between various other concepts such as constant acceleration, velocity, position, and time. These relationships need to be clearly identified in statement form.

MATHEMATICS

Topic: Monomials and Polynomials

The critical attribute of a monomial would be: a numeral, variable, or indirect product of a numeral and one or more variables.

Examples of this concept would be:

-6, $8b3$, x

Non-example:

$\frac{-8}{x}$ (The variable is in the denominator.)

Next, the teacher might teach the concept of "polynomials." The two critical attributes would be: (1) a mathematical expression which (2) consists of two or more terms. Some examples would be:

$7a + b$

$3a + b + 2c$

One particular type of polynomial (a subconcept) is a "binomial." The critical attribute of a binomial is that it consists of two terms:

$a + 4$

The critical attribute of the concept "trinomial" is that it must contain three terms:

$3a2 + 2a + 4$

Topic: Complementary and Supplementary Angles

A teacher would teach the concept of "complementary angles" by emphasizing the two critical attributes: (1) there must be two angles, and (2) the sum of the two angles must equal 90°. Following is an example and a non-example of complementary angles:

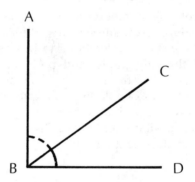

<ABC and <CBD are complementary.

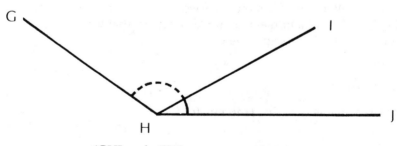

<GHI and <IHJ are not complementary.

The concept of "supplementary angles" would have the following two critical attributes: (1) there must be two angles, and (2) the sum of the two angles must equal 180°.

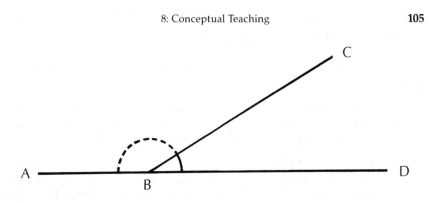

<ABC and <CBD are supplementary.

Topic: Equations

A teacher who is introducing the basic concept of an "equation" would emphasize the following critical attributes:

1. Numbers and/or letters represent numbers.
2. An equal sign is used to separate two sides of the mathematical sentence or equation.
3. Both sides of the equation must have an equal value.

As the teacher proceeds to teach the concept of an equation, he or she might realize that students do not understand a related subconcept, such as "sides" of an equation. At this point it would be necessary to stop teaching about equations and back up to focus on the concept of "sides" of an equation until the students are clear on this related subconcept. The teacher could then resume teaching about the main concept, equations.

To teach graphing, it is necessary to identify several concepts related to this topic. These might include concepts such as "plane," "co-ordinate," "axis," "quadrant," "intercept," "abscissa," and "ordinate."

The sequence of concepts must be decided on by the teacher, then examples and non-examples of each concept can be presented. Finally, students could learn how some of these concepts relate to one another through making graphs.

Many math texts include written objectives. It is essential to clarify and emphasize the principle students must understand in order to achieve the objective as stated in the text. Unfortunately, many texts spell out what students will *do*, but fail to identify what students must *learn* — the main understanding. If the text fails to identify the main learning objective, then the teacher must do so.

GEOGRAPHY: LATITUDE AND LONGITUDE

A learning objective or main understanding about the concepts of latitude and longitude could be written as follows:

> Lines of latitude which run east-west measure distance north and south of the equator, whereas lines of longitude which run north-south measure distance east and west of the Prime Meridian.

It is difficult to learn two concepts at once. A teacher needs to teach one concept before moving on to the next one. For example, you might teach the concept of latitude by looking at examples, finding locations along lines of latitude, and calculating distances north and south of the equator. Only after students have a clear understanding of latitude would the teacher move on to the next concept, longitude. Once both concepts have been taught, students would then be able to see the connection between latitude and longitude to locate places on a grid or map.

MATHEMATICS: FRACTIONS AND DECIMALS

A main understanding in math could be written as follows:

> Both fractions (which represent part of the whole) and decimals (which represent parts out of 100) may be used interchangeably to represent proportion.

To teach this main understanding, a teacher must first ensure that students understand the basic concepts of "fraction" and "decimal."

If the students do not understand both concepts, they will not understand the relationship between the two.

ART: THE VANISHING POINT

A teacher wants to teach the concept of the "vanishing point" in drawing. In planning the lesson focusing on this concept, a teacher might think through the following things:

The critical attribute is: (1) two or more lines converging to a single point.

A main understanding about the vanishing point could be:

> The use of the vanishing point on a two-dimensional sheet of paper creates the illusion of a three-dimensional object.

This main understanding could be broken down further:

1. The further from the vanishing point, the greater the apparent size of the object.
2. The closer to the vanishing point, the smaller the apparent size of the object.

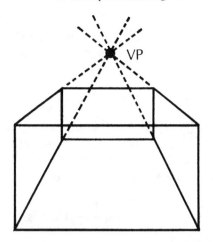

A note about this example: Normally a teacher would identify a main understanding, and then identify related concepts within it. In this instance, however, the teacher identified a main concept first — the vanishing point — then wrote two main understandings about the vanishing point. These are subunderstandings of the major concept.

HISTORY: CONFLICT

The major concept being taught in a History lesson might be "conflict." The teacher would decide which main understandings about conflict to teach, using examples from history. The historical examples used to illustrate some important principles about conflict (drawn from the French-English conflict in North America prior to 1800) could be:

1. Expansion in an arena of limited resources and space leads to conflict.
2. Britain and France established Indian allies which helped maintain each nation's control of the fur trade.
3. Conflict in Europe between colonial powers spilled over into conflict in the New World.
4. Through conflict, Britain ultimately gained supremacy over France in the struggle for imperialistic control in North America.

SUMMARY

It is the interplay among facts, concepts, and main understandings that helps students cluster important ideas and principles which enable them to organize knowledge in a meaningful way.

Teachers who emphasize a conceptual approach to teaching begin their planning around the major concepts they wish to teach. These concepts become a base from which to determine what facts and main understandings need to be learned by students.

A teacher must be able to help students define concepts on the basis of some common ground, otherwise confusion and uncertainty results. Clear and precise teaching overcomes this confusion.

PLANNING AND LEARNING

Planning (what a teacher does) is a different process from learning (what a student does). Up to this point most of our school experience has been that of a student. Now we are going to become teachers, so it is necessary to think like a teacher — a planner.

FIGURE 8.2
LEARNING AND PLANNING PROCESSES

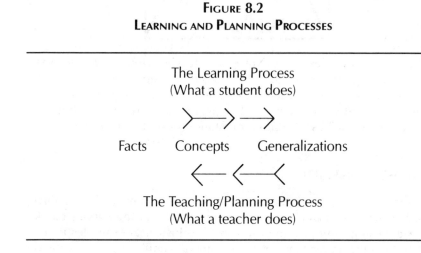

The Learning Process
(What a student does)

Facts   Concepts   Generalizations

The Teaching/Planning Process
(What a teacher does)

Teachers who fail to understand the relationships between facts, concepts, and main understandings tend to employ a style of teaching which emphasizes memorization of trivia and isolated detail.

Chapter Nine:
MORE APPROACHES TO INSTRUCTION

MAIN UNDERSTANDINGS

In this chapter you will learn the following:

1. A teacher's selection of an instructional model is determined by the students' needs, the teacher's preferences, the time and materials available, intended learning outcomes, and curriculum.
2. Each approach to instruction, although discrete in many respects, may overlap with other approaches.
3. To meet the broad needs and learning styles of students, a teacher must possess a repertoire of instructional approaches.
4. Teachers must adapt instruction to suit specific subjects and specialized areas.

AREAS OF FOCUS IN THE CLASSROOM

Teachers who can draw from a variety of instructional approaches will be able to meet the needs of many different kinds of students with different styles of learning. For example, a teacher may *show* the area of a triangle with a diagram, *tell* students how to apply the area formula, then have students *handle* various geometric shapes as they apply the formula to concrete materials.

There are three major areas of focus for a lesson, each of which requires a different teaching approach. If the objective is to teach content, then the instructional models categorized under the content or informational focus would be appropriate.

If the teacher wants to develop a more positive classroom environment or to develop interpersonal skills among students, a teaching approach in which group skills, interactions, and interpersonal bonding could be enhanced, models with a co-operative or interactive focus would be appropriate.

If a teacher decides that the most important objective is to help students gain self-esteem, models with a personal, individualized focus would be appropriate.

FIGURE 9.1
SELECTING A TEACHING APPROACH

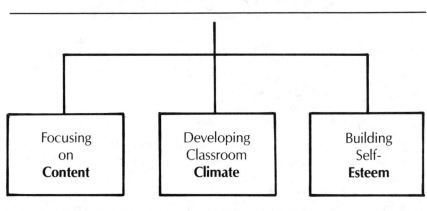

A teacher cannot focus on all the models at one time. She or he must decide which model to draw on, depending on whether the primary purpose is to teach content, create a co-operative climate, or build students' self-esteem.

FIGURE 9.2
AREA OF FOCUS

Teacher   Student(s)

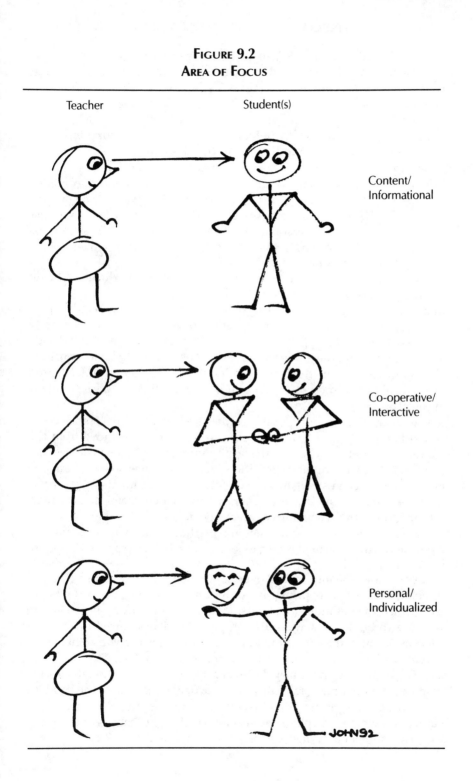

Content/
Informational

Co-operative/
Interactive

Personal/
Individualized

JOHN92

As indicated in Figure 9.2, in the content/information area of focus, the teacher imparts knowledge to the student. In the co-operative/ interactive focus, the teacher creates a situation in which students co-operate and interact with one another under the watchful eye of the teacher. In the personal/individualized area of focus, the teacher looks beyond students' masks to perceive the real needs, aspirations, and accomplishments of each individual in the classroom.

The appropriate focus changes over time and with different students. With a new class, a teacher might focus on the content and information because it is important to get students working right from the beginning. Teachers in higher grades often begin with the content focus because they do not know the personal backgrounds of students. Focus on co-operative/interactive processes or personal/individualized development might be more appropriately left for later.

On the other hand, a teacher in the early grades might decide to begin teaching from the personal/individualized focus. The teacher might feel that it is most important to learn the names of the students and to play a variety of support games or activities in which the teacher gets to know each student in a positive manner. Next, this teacher could decide to use models from the group/interactive focus in order to build a positive classroom climate. In this case, models from the content/information focus would be appropriate after children had adjusted to one another in the classroom.

The teacher's perception of the students is always important. If some students are not participating in class, a teacher might move from the content/information focus to the group/interactive focus. The teacher could return to a content/information focus later, once some interactive bridges have been established among students. If students fight, argue, or make racist remarks, a teacher might switch from the content/ information to the co-operative/interactive focus.

Figure 9.3 illustrates that teaching methods and activities may be associated with a particular area of focus, but can take place within more than one area of focus.

For example, the inquiry/discovery approach can be used in a teacher-directed lesson that is primarily content/informational, as students are led toward the solution or conclusion, or with student groups who are working through the stages of an inquiry. Student-centred instruction such as resource-based co-operative learning can involve either individual work or group work. It can incorporate whole-class conceptual learning as well as an inquiry/discovery approach. Even though aspects of another model may be built into a particular approach, the models, nevertheless, are outlined as discrete teaching methods to provide a basis upon which to explore and test alternative approaches to teaching. Generic approaches to instruction are outlined in Figure 9.4.

FIGURE 9.3

METHODS AND ACTIVITIES WITHIN THE AREAS OF FOCUS

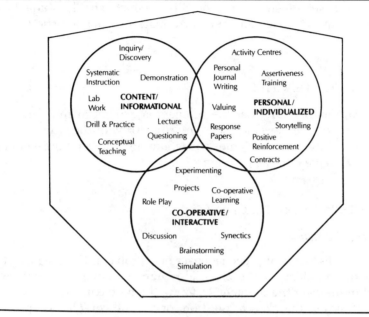

FIGURE 9.4

GENERIC APPROACHES TO INSTRUCTION

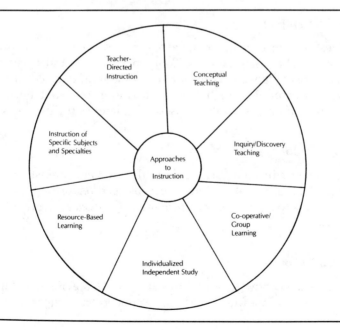

THE INQUIRY/DISCOVERY MODEL

Inquiry is a set of steps or procedures which enable students to investigate and discover on their own, instead of having the teacher tell them.

ROLE OF THE TEACHER

The teacher makes sure that the problem is defined in the same way by all students, then becomes a co-investigator with the students. The teacher's job is to probe with more questions and to offer more evidence as students delve into the problem.

STAGES IN INQUIRY TEACHING

Define the Problem

The inquiry/discovery approach focuses on a problem. The teacher often defines the problem for the class, although sometimes students will suggest or discover the problem. Defining the problem may be a simple matter of asking the class a question, or a more complicated process in which some discussion and explanation is necessary before the problem is clearly defined.

Gather Information

Ask questions, test, evaluate, measure, and compare and contrast the information. This information will be checked out and verified when there is more evidence to consider. In simple inquiry/discovery lessons, such as the example which follows, this step may not be necessary because the information will be discovered later in the process.

Develop Hypotheses

Students make educated guesses about the problem, brainstorm possible solutions, look at initial evidence such as pictures or objects, or apply new materials to a scientific experiment. Inferences are drawn from this information.

Test Each Hypothesis

More evidence is now provided to students. This evidence helps them judge whether or not the hypotheses were correct or incorrect.

Arrive at a Solution or Conclusion

This final step is a natural outgrowth of testing the various hypotheses. Remind students that the conclusion they have drawn is tentative and based on only the available evidence. The solution (in this approach to teaching) is the learning objective of the lesson. Students inquire into the problem and discover the solution. This approach teaches thinking skills and motivates students to learn.

EXAMPLE OF A DISCOVERY/INQUIRY-ORIENTED LESSON: THE LEGEND OF SEDNA

Problem

In the Inuit legend of Sedna, goddess of the sea, an umiak (boat) was overcrowded, and it was decided that Sedna should be left behind on shore. However, Sedna swam to the umiak and clung to its sides. Her father, fearing that Sedna would cause the umiak to capsize, demanded that she let go. She did not. What could the father do?

Develop Hypotheses

Students could create hypotheses such as (a) let her continue to cling to the boat, (b) return to land, (c) push her away from the umiak, etc. The students will be motivated to find solutions because they want to find out what actually happened to Sedna.

Test the Hypotheses

To test the hypotheses, the teacher would say, "Turn the page and read what happened in the legend." According to the legend, the father cut off Sedna's fingers, sending her to the bottom of the sea.

Solution/Conclusion

Sedna became the goddess of the sea and her amputated fingers were transformed into arctic sea mammals such as the seal, walrus, and whale. According to Inuit mythology, Sedna held power over sea life. Early Inuit customs paid homage to Sedna so she would look favourably upon hunters and fishermen, enabling them to return home safely and with bounty from the sea.

Students could conclude that, in early Inuit culture, sacrifice for the common good was a desirable trait. (Sedna was sacrificed to save those in the umiak.) Subsequent discussion could focus on the relevance of this value in contemporary society.

This example showed how the inquiry/discovery approach might be used in a Language Arts/English lesson. In Social Studies, students might investigate the economic worth of resources and then test their hypotheses by looking at charts and graphs. Primary school children might examine a picture and try to infer such things as "What time of day is it?" "Where are the people going?" "What are they doing?" Then the teacher could provide further information to enable students to verify whether or not their hypotheses were correct.

INQUIRY/DISCOVERY BASED ON DISCREPANT INFORMATION

Have you ever aspired to be a magician? The "twenty questions" format of inductive teaching may give you the chance. First, prepare students by telling them that their role will be to explain what happens at the "magic" moment and why it happens. They will ask questions about what they observed. You will provide only "yes" or "no" answers. After asking questions and listening to their peers, students are often able to arrive at the generalization which explains the discrepant information.

You could demonstrate a discrepant event such as the water diffusion experiment. In this example, you show the students two matching large beakers, each three-quarters filled with water. Next you show two matching small beakers also nearly filled with water.

Place three drops of food colouring in each of the small beakers. The liquid in each should turn a uniform colour.

Now set one of the small beakers into each of the large beakers. In one of the large beakers, water from the smaller one diffuses and colours the liquid in the larger beaker. But in the other large beaker, the liquid does not change colour after the small beaker has been immersed in it. Why not? Why did the water diffuse in one case but not in the other?

Students would then ask questions, which you would answer with "yes" or "no" until they reach a conclusion. Have you determined why there was a difference in the diffusion of the colour? Think about water temperature.

Another use of discrepant information would be to show students excerpts from two inconsistent campaign speeches delivered by the same politician. Why would a politician offer contradictory messages? Possible hypotheses might be: "He or she changed political parties." "They occurred at different times in the person's life." "The speeches were addressed to different audiences." After hypothesizing, student would then read (or be told) the reason(s) for the differences.

An inquiry/discovery lesson for elementary school children would be to show them pictures of the same city, one set portraying the city as a wealthy and beautiful place and the other set portraying it as poor, old, and dirty. What might explain the difference? Hypotheses could be: "The pictures were taken in different seasons, in different years, or in different parts of the city."

The Co-Operative or Group Learning Model

In co-operative learning, students are required to work together to achieve a common goal. Social goals are combined with academic work. Students brainstorm and build creatively on one another's ideas. Students can be encouraged to be interdependent by sharing resources with other group members.

Seating arrangements which facilitate face-to-face interaction (often circles work best) help students hear many points of view.

Some students cannot work in a group at first. They either dominate the group or sit passively and contribute very little. They do not co-operate with others. In group situations, students can practise the skill of co-operation.

In brief, the goals of co-operative learning are positive interdependence, face-to-face interaction, individual and group accountability, and development of social and academic abilities.

ROLE OF THE TEACHER

In co-operative learning, the teacher plays a non-directive role. When students are helping each other, the teacher is free to observe students and assist them if necessary. Students are given time to control their own learning process.

SEQUENCE OF ACTIVITIES

The following are the steps involved in a group project.

1. Identify the topic to be investigated.
2. Emphasize a social skill. The skill may be suggested by the class or the teacher. "Participation," "co-operation," and "respect" are examples. The social skill word is placed as a heading on the chalkboard, and students are asked to describe what the social skill "sounds like" and "looks like." The "sounds like" suggestions are listed on the left and the "looks like" suggestions on the right. For example:

Respect

Sounds Like	Looks Like
"I'll follow you."	Taking turns.
"Your idea is different but good."	Listening to each other.
"Liking others."	Giving back things you borrow.

3. Organize research groups. Group students in clusters of three or four. The groups may comprise students who are of mixed ability, of matched ability, or randomly selected.

   Roles such as chairperson, recorder, reporter, and social skills monitor may be assigned. The social skills monitor would tabulate the number of times group members used their social skills.
4. The teacher gives the class directions regarding the task, materials, room arrangement, and criteria for success in both academic and social skills. The teacher also stresses that each student is responsible for creating a part of the group learning experience.
5. The groups collect and analyze information, with help from the teacher when necessary. The teacher or students monitor the social interaction of each group. Informal notes or observation checklists may be used.
6. Student representatives from each group report orally or turn in a written assignment.
7. The teacher and class discuss the shared learning with the group, and evaluate the academic learning process.
8. The teacher and class evaluate the social learning process. Students are asked how they felt about the activity, what worked well, and what changes could be made to improve their co-operative social skills next time.

THE JIGSAW

The jigsaw is a co-operative learning activity that is frequently used in schools. It provides a structure for co-operative student interaction and an interactive means for students to acquire and present information. It gives students a unique chance to read, speak, listen, and encourage the learning of others.

If students have not previously done a jigsaw, the teacher might say:

In this class we will be using a team approach to acquire information about a topic. You will be assigned to a "home team." Then you will be reorganized into an "expert (specific information) group." Each member of the home team will develop expertise concerning a specific piece of information (a piece of the jigsaw) by working in an "expert" group.

After learning the information, you will return to your home team. Each of your home-team members will teach their "expert" knowledge to the group. We call this approach a jigsaw because you won't know the whole picture until each home-team member provides you with their piece of the jigsaw.

Each home-team member is responsible for the expert knowledge of the entire home team.

The teacher would also remind students:

I will provide key questions to guide your study, peer teaching, and mutual reviewing. Assignments will be distributed later. Evaluation will be based on your individual mark and a mark for the collective learning of your home team.

The teacher would then outline details of team formation, work stations, expected classroom behaviour, and the topic itself.

In summary, the sequence of activities is:

1. Introduce topic and study questions.
2. Assign students to home teams.
3. Re-assign home-team members to "expert" groups.
4. Provide information and materials for each "expert" team.
5. Organize and learn the content with the expert group.
6. Regroup into the original home teams.
7. Experts teach the home team their part of the information.
8. Evaluate and reward home teams with some recognition.

CLASS OR GROUP DISCUSSIONS

Class or group discussions led by a skilful teacher can be used to learn new ideas, adjust attitudes, solve problems, develop communication skills, and increase sensitivity to others' points of view. A small-group discussion led by a student chairperson is another example of co-operative or group learning. The following are guidelines for organizing a group or class discussion.

- Set time limits.
- Communicate the topic and its boundaries.
- Provide some background upon which students can draw: individual or small-group work beforehand, writing a position paper, or reading material on the topic.
- Communicate the purpose of the discussion.
- Set ground rules.
- Begin with a springboard for focus and interest: a quote, poem, anecdote, film, picture, role play, hypothetical incident, or series of open-ended questions.

- Keep the group members on the topic. Restate the problem, summarize, redirect the trend of the discussion through direct statements or guide questions.
- Stop any off-topic, immaterial, emotional, or negative discussions.

The following teaching techniques will contribute to effective discussions.

- Lead rather than monopolize.
- Offer personal opinions only after the group members have exhausted their views and comments.
- Keep the discussion moving at a fast pace.
- Refocus the group to keep everyone on topic.
- Encourage everyone to participate. Establish an open atmosphere.
- Encourage new ideas.
- Avoid judgmental statements.
- Use open-ended questions such as "Would anyone like to comment?" "What do you think?" "What else might we say?" "Who has another idea?" "How could you add to this idea?"
- Relate the discussion to the students' personal experience.
- Clarify issues and options.
- Summarize at appropriate times.
- Accept comments made by students.
- Bring the discussion to a close. Summarize, emphasize the main point(s); raise new questions or unanswered aspects of the topic.

BENEFITS OF CO-OPERATIVE LEARNING

1. Academic achievement is increased. Each student can piggyback on the ideas of others and learn by teaching others.
2. Students' self-esteem is improved as they develop a sense of belonging to a group. They become more willing to share ideas with one another.
3. Multicultural differences are lessened. All ideas are valued. Positive attitudes increase, particularly when the co-operative group effort results in achievement of the task with an accompanying high mark, record, or sense of achievement.
4. Students' personal and social skills improve.

LIMITATIONS OF CO-OPERATIVE LEARNING

1. Curriculum materials are often inadequate. Most texts are written for individual and competitive achievement. Teachers must prepare many of their own materials for co-operative learning.
2. Independent-minded students may prefer to work by themselves.

3. Unless monitored, more able students will do the work for poorer students.
4. Parents or guardians and students who see only the academic aspect of school and not the interpersonal/co-operative skills dimensions may complain that the work is not sufficiently challenging.
5. Co-operative learning is more time-consuming than an individually oriented and teacher-directed approach.

THE INDEPENDENT STUDY MODEL

For many years learning contracts and learning packages have been developed by teachers for independent study. Activity centres/learning stations are also forms of independent study. In recent years computerized instruction has become a valued source for independent learning.

COMPUTERIZED INSTRUCTION

The use of computers in the classroom is increasing. Some schools have linked into electronic mail networks in which classes can communicate with their local or distant counterparts. Design work can be done on school computers. Frogs and insects can be dissected by computer simulation. Students can search library catalogue files for information. Mathematical formulas, charts, and graphs can be constructed and used for analytic purposes. The following are some of the uses of computers in the classroom.

- Drill and practice. Offers review of basic facts and terminology, questions and answers.
- Tutorial. Presents new information and concepts. Gives remedial instruction and feedback. Students can ask and answer questions. Monitors the student's responses.
- Games. Motivational drill and practice. Students compete against the computer. Offers learning of facts, skills, strategies.
- Simulations. Based on realistic situations. Help students develop decision-making skills. Computer tells consequences of decisions.
- Inquiry/Discovery. Allows students to test hypotheses using the inductive approach. Trial and error. Students analyze data. Permits search procedures. Develops principles and rules.
- Problem-solving. Variables can be manipulated and calculations performed.

LEARNING CONTRACTS

Greater student responsibility for individualized learning can occur through learning contracts. Students agree to do a certain amount and quality of work in exchange for a contracted mark. The teacher, in consultation with each student or group of students, designs a written contract which all parties sign.

A learning contract should include the following:

- Objectives
- Required activities
- Optional activities, if any
- Written study guide for each activity
- Student decision on how to meet the requirements
- Student decision on when to meet the requirements
- Signatures of student and teacher

FIGURE 9.5
SAMPLE LEARNING CONTRACT

Student's name _____

Date to be completed _____

a. Read Chapter 4.
b. Read two assigned handouts.
c. Saw the wood.
d. Cut the wood.
e. Nail and glue the pieces together.
f. Paint the stool.
g. Pass the test on the woodwork unit.

SIGNED _____ (Student)

APPROVED _____ (Teacher)

COMPLETED _____ (Teacher)

LEARNING PACKAGES

Learning packages are designed for individual self-instruction. There are some commercially available materials, but most are teacher-made materials uniquely developed to meet the needs of the curriculum and individual students.

A learning package should contain the following:

- Overview
- Rationale for students
- Objectives
- Content to learn
- Exercises/problems/activities
- Study guide
  - Instructions
  - Sources for materials
- Self-correcting tests
- Final test
- Student judgments on what was learned

The Resource-Based Learning Model

ROLE OF THE TEACHER

In this model, the role of the teacher is mainly that of a resource provider. Some guidance, of course, is needed to help students learn effectively and efficiently from the resources. This model brings a wide range of appropriate print and non-print media to bear on instruction. Teachers should locate, evaluate, select, and use media in their classrooms. School librarians often provide highly valued help with this approach.

The teacher would begin by examining the materials available in the school resource centre, then those available from the school district. If necessary, the teacher could also order resources from sources outside the school district (*e.g.*, Ministry of Education, National Film Board, businesses, and voluntary organizations). Selecting resources is an ongoing process — over time, the teacher will develop a file of resources (pictures, articles, etc.) for future reference.

ACTIVITY CENTRES OR LEARNING STATIONS

Activity centres are areas in a classroom where students may participate in self-directed learning activities. Materials in an activity centre are varied: worksheets, audiovisual kits, activity cards, photographs, crossword puzzles, maps, books, etc. There may be several "stations" in the centre which focus on various aspects of the main theme.

A centre may be a special-interest centre, or it may serve to reinforce knowledge and skills taught in regular classroom lessons. It may be set up for purposes of remedial work and review for some students, or enrichment for others. Skill development — listening, finding information, writing — can be a major purpose.

Centres are student-centred, encourage active participation, and eliminate or reduce many of the discipline problems found in conventional classrooms. Every activity in the centre must have a worthwhile learning purpose, and this purpose must be clearly identified for students.

Location

Centres may be located on a table at the back of the room, along the side windows, on the teacher's desk, on a bulletin board, or hanging as a mobile from the ceiling, tree branches, or a wooden support structure. Tables and benches serve as centre locations. A welcome sign or theme should be attractively displayed to draw students to the centre.

Materials

There are no limits to the kinds or numbers of materials, both primary and secondary, that may be used. For example, worksheet pages, objects, pictures, microscopes, aquariums, and audiovisual materials are appropriate.

Objectives

Overall objectives should be spelled out for students, as well as the objectives for individual activities within the centre or station.

Instructions

Directions should be concise, self-explanatory, and clearly displayed. There should be directions available for each activity or station within the centre as well as overall directions for use of the centre.

Self-Marking

Immediate feedback is most meaningful, and even the youngest students quickly accept the responsibility of checking out their answers. Unless undue pressure is placed on students, they will respond positively and honestly to checking their own work in the centre.

Monitoring System

The teacher needs to know how well students are doing, how many have finished, and whether it is time to add more materials or change themes in the activity centre.

Displaying a wall chart of students' progress is *not* a good idea — it could be detrimental to some students' motivation and self-esteem. It is preferable to have students check off work on individual record sheets. They may hand in completed work or place it in a collection box. Sign-in/sign-out sheets are frequently used.

USING MEDIA IN THE CLASSROOM

Use a wide variety of media to support instruction (*e.g.*, videotape, computer-assisted instruction, film, audiotape, slide-tape presentations, overhead transparencies, models, simulations, video recorders, and games).

Use media to:

- Introduce a topic
- Motivate students about a topic
- Develop a particular aspect of a topic
- Deliver the bulk of content for a lesson
- Review a topic previously covered in a class
- Evaluate an individual's performance
- Provide individualized instruction to some or all students
- Allow some students to work independently

PROJECT WORK USING THE SCHOOL RESOURCE CENTRE

When a lesson or unit requires the acquisition and processing of information, the school library or learning resources centre is the source of that information.

The following procedures will help in planning project work:

- First, do some preplanning. Find out from the teacher-librarian what print and audiovisual materials are available for the subject or topic being covered.
- Express your teacher goal in terms of information to be acquired and processed. (What information is needed? What will students do with it?)
- Brainstorm with students the student assignment or problem to be completed, resolved, or solved.
- Discuss with students the kinds of information that will be required to achieve the objective. (What kinds of questions do we need to answer? What kinds of information do we need?)

- Discuss with students how the research should be organized. (Each student independently? As part of a small group? As part of the whole class?)
- Determine what library and research skills students will need (consult with the teacher-librarian).
- Determine the time required to complete the research. (One class period, or more?)
- Discuss with students how the resolution or solution is best presented. (As a written or oral report? As a group or class discussion and decision? As a poster, chart, videotape, etc., prepared by the individual, group or class?)
- Engage in follow-up discussion with students. How useful were the materials used for research? What did we learn? Are there questions which are still unanswered? What conclusions can be made? How do you feel about the information?

PROS AND CONS OF RESOURCE-BASED LEARNING

Like other methods, resource-based learning has potential weaknesses of which teachers need to be aware. Resource units can become unnecessarily time-consuming. There needs to be co-ordination with other staff members to avoid overlap with topics in other grades. Continued monitoring of student work is required. Finally, remember that resource-based learning means that power is shared. The teacher will no longer be at centre stage. Students will be responsible for their own learning as they work through a variety of sources.

INSTRUCTION OF SPECIAL SUBJECTS AND SPECIALTIES

Basic approaches to instruction eventually must be applied to subject needs. The lists that follow provide guidelines for the effective teaching of specific subjects and areas of concern.

KINDERGARTEN

Emotional Development

- Engage in activities with initiative and confidence
- Remain absorbed in task to completion
- Accept responsibility for their own behaviour
- Accept constructive criticism
- Accept differences in others

Social Development

The teacher encourages students to:

• Value oneself
• Work co-operatively with others
• Be sensitive to the rights and feelings of others
• Participate in groups

Physical Development

The teacher encourages students to:

• Participate in gross motor activities (running, jumping, and throwing)
• Participate in fine motor activities (cutting, drawing, stringing)
• Respond to emotions and music with movement

Intellectual Development

The teacher encourages students to:

• Make meaning through play by exploring, testing, representing, and learning about the physical world
• Express ideas and feelings through dramatic play, enjoying music, exploring art materials, and sharing stories
• Express curiosity about concrete objects, events, or relationships

LITERACY LEARNING IN THE PRIMARY GRADES

The teacher encourages students to:

• Talk to learn and share
• Share literature for enjoyment and information in pairs, small groups, or large groups
• Collaborate in experiences which enrich concepts, vocabulary, and language structures
• Write to explore ideas and clarify thinking
• Model reading and writing "meaning-making" strategies
• Write in a variety of formats (stories, poems, reports, letters, journals, learning logs, memoirs, literary genres, etc.)
• Explore a range of reading materials (charts, library or trade books, reading texts, reference books, group books, magazines and newspapers)
• Use Art, Music, Drama, media for building, responding, and extending meaning-making in literacy learning
• Evaluate literacy learning through daily samples of student work

SPECIAL NEEDS STUDENTS

Teachers need to demonstrate:

- Patience
- Sense of humour
- Positive outlook, being encouraging and cheerful
- Awareness that *all* students in the classroom are their responsibility
- An ability to create an accepting environment
- A good language model
- Knowledge of a variety of methods for teaching basic skills
- Flexibility in finding creative ways to circumvent handicap
- Co-operation with other teachers in peer coaching and teacher assistance teams (TAT), and with resource teachers (teacher-librarians)

PHYSICAL EDUCATION

The teacher needs to provide:

- Motor skill development
- Active participation for all
- Concept-based instruction
- Positive relationships with others
- Joy of movement
- Clear directions
- A variety of clearly defined tasks
- Full demonstration of activities
- Appropriate and accurate cues
- Specific congruent feedback

SOCIAL STUDIES

The teacher needs to utilize:

- An interdisciplinary approach
- A conceptual approach
- Analysis of historical and current issues
- A focus on values and feelings
- An inquiry/discovery approach
- A focus on past, present, and future
- Personal, community, societal, and global perspectives
- Relationships among social phenomena
- A personal connection between content and students' lives and experiences

CORE FRENCH

The teacher needs to:

- Establish a warm and accepting atmosphere
- Create lively and well-paced lessons
- Prepare a complete lesson plan with a warm-up activity, a review, the presentation of new material, a main activity, and a concluding activity
- Design communicative activities that promote listening, speaking, reading, and writing
- Present a good model for spoken French
- Provide opportunities for frequent practice
- Promote a deeper knowledge and acceptance of francophone cultures
- Correct errors tactfully
- Use English only when necessary

MATHEMATICS

The teacher needs to utilize:

- A discovery approach
- The development of understanding
- Concrete materials
- Real-world problems
- Problem-solving approaches
- The use of calculators and computers
- Mental computation and instrumentation
- Intermediate algorithms
- Opportunities to relate math to other subjects
- The various fields of Math — Algebra, Geometry, Trigonometry, Co-ordinate Geometry, Functions

SCIENCE

The teacher should:

- Encourage confidence through a positive classroom environment
- Help students structure their *own* personal knowledge
- Embed subject matter in everyday life situations
- Convey an authentic image of science
- Include an inquiry/discovery approach
- Deal with values related to scientific literacy
- Clarify characteristics of scientific literacy
- Promote critical thinking and use of science process skills

ART EDUCATION

The teacher should:

- Provide an opportunity for students to develop perceptual awareness through observation, image-making, and tactile experiences
- Demonstrate techniques using a variety of materials in two and three dimensions
- Encourage students to explore media in a unique and personal way
- Introduce artworks and artists from various cultures, using a wide variety of materials such as slides, reproductions, films, videotapes, print materials, actual works of art, and visits from artists
- Encourage students to look for examples of artistic expression in their community and elsewhere, including situations not usually associated with the arts
- Organize opportunities for students to talk about their own artwork and the works of other artists
- Develop with students criteria for evaluating their own and others' artwork

LANGUAGE ARTS (ELEMENTARY)

The teacher should:

- Encourage student-teacher interaction and student-student interaction
- Listen and respond to students
- Use open-ended questioning
- Require students to write individually, in pairs, and in groups
- Write him or herself
- Encourage students to share their writing
- Encourage student reading
- Read to students
- Require students to respond to what they read in various ways (writing, talking, drama, various media)
- Organize students to work in pairs, small groups, or large groups
- Model correct language use (speaking, writing, reading, listening)

ENGLISH (SECONDARY)

The teacher should:

- Organize students to ensure that they respond to what they read
- Encourage students to discuss their language use
- Write and share with students

- Read and respond to what he or she reads
- Ensure that students respond in various modes (speaking, listening, reading, writing, drama, media)
- Provide opportunities for students to share and discuss their writing among themselves
- Model correct language use (speaking, writing, reading, listening)
- Use questions to initiate, extend, probe, and discuss
- Use a variety of literature (novels, short stories, plays, poetry, journalism, popular print, cartoons, etc.)
- Provide opportunities for student self-selection of topics for writing and reading

Part IV: CLASSROOM INTERACTIONS

Chapter Ten:
QUESTIONING AND RESPONDING

MAIN UNDERSTANDINGS

In this chapter you will learn the following:

1. Teachers should practise their skills in asking questions.
2. Questions can be used to evaluate, capture students' attention, and promote learning in the classroom.
3. Effective teachers develop a repertoire of types and levels of questions to enhance their students' thinking skills.
4. The way in which we respond to students has a direct impact on their behaviour and learning.
5. Positive teacher responses to students may be verbal or non-verbal.

QUESTIONING

Think back to when you were a student. Did teachers' questions make you feel good or inadequate, confused or motivated? Whatever the feeling, teachers, students, and questions go together. This chapter explores the process of questioning from the perspectives of teacher and students.

THE IMPORTANCE OF TEACHER QUESTIONS

Most teachers use "key questions" throughout a lesson to *see if students understand* the material. Writing key questions beforehand helps teachers focus on the main ideas of their lesson.

Teachers also use questions to *measure progress* — for example, an oral quiz at the end of a unit, a spelling test to check new vocabulary, or summary questions at the end of a lesson. Examples of such questions are: "Does everyone understand the assignment?" "Who could explain the importance of this circle to the Plains Indians?" "Will someone demonstrate that badminton serve?"

Questions are used for diagnosis. For example, you might have to ask questions to ascertain the knowledge and ability of a transfer student who arrives without a record of previous accomplishment. Or you may discover that illiteracy has prevented students from successfully completing tests for which advanced reading skills were required.

Questions are used to *determine entry level* to a grade or to a new section of work.

Questions can *enrich a lesson*. "What if . . .?" or "Imagine . . ." or "How is a Hamlet like a used-car salesman?" are enrichment questions.

Another purpose of questions is to *engage students* in the class as teachers invite them to act on and think through what is being taught. Students create their own personal understandings when they are active participants.

Questions give students opportunities to *practise the oral and written responses* needed by citizens of a democracy.

Questions *influence students' motivation, self-esteem,* and *classroom management*. Can you think of some questions that would fulfil these functions?

TYPES OF QUESTIONS

One way to categorize questions is on the basis of levels of thinking. Questions may also be categorized as broad or narrow, convergent or divergent (open or closed), and probing/extending.

Broad and Narrow Questions

Broad questions enable students to respond from a variety of perspectives. Although this permits a wide variation in response, it is difficult to judge the suitability of the students' responses. For example, the question "What do you think about building a new skating arena in our community?" may serve to initiate discussion, but it is so broad that the discussion could go in almost any direction. It is difficult for students to know where to begin or what aspect to focus on, in order to respond adequately to broadly worded assignments.

Narrow questions lead students toward a major idea or understanding, or relate to some previous information. For example, the teacher could give students the formula $H_2 + CL_2 = 2HCL$, then ask a series of related narrow questions, such as: "How many molecules of hydrogen chloride can be formed using one molecule of hydrogen?" "How many molecules of hydrogen chloride can be formed from one molecule of hydrogen gas?" "How many molecules of chlorine gas would be needed to produce eight molecules of hydrogen chloride?"

Convergent and Divergent Questions

Convergent (or closed) questions have a single answer. Divergent (or open) questions have several possible answers. Questions beginning with "How many . . .?", "Where is . . .?", or "Who is . . .?" are convergent questions, as are "Why do plants stretch toward sunlight?" and "What is x in the equation $x^2 = 49$?"

The following are examples of divergent questions: "What might be the meaning of this cartoon?" "How could you measure the distance between two points separated by a large grove of trees?" "How do people stay warm during Canadian winters?"

For teaching factual material, a series of convergent questions are more appropriate. If the teacher wants students to express their ideas, feelings, or interpretations, then divergent questions are more appropriate.

Values Questions

Values questions require students to draw on their own values and feelings. Some examples of values questions are: "Should a bridge be built in this location?" "Is ——— worthwhile?" "Can you prioritize these things?" "Which is better?"

Probing / Extending Questions

Probing/extending questions are designed to lead students deeper into the topic under discussion. They are backup questions to an initial question about the topic. The following are examples of probing/extending questions: "How else could you do this?" "What else?" "Can you think of some alternatives?" "If this occurred, then what might happen?" "What is the next step?"

Probing/extending questions should form a pattern. A typical pattern is to move from lower-level questions to higher-level questions, leading students toward an understanding of the topic.

This type of questioning can be used in dialogues between the teacher and one student, or in discussions involving the teacher and the whole class.

LEVELS OF QUESTIONS

Questions can be used to challenge students to think. Thinking may be simple or sophisticated, and the level of thinking by students in the classroom often is guided by the level of question asked by the teacher. A simple one-answer question is correspondingly simple to answer. Complex or sophisticated questions require higher levels of thinking.

Examples of lower-level ("fact" or "memory") questions are "What is the name of the street?" or "Where was the firefighter when the alarm sounded?" They can often be answered with a word or phrase.

Examples of higher-level ("thinking") questions are "Why does more rain fall on this side of the mountains?" or "Did the bank robbers make the best decision?" Higher-level questions require students to respond in sentences. These questions require more time and effort from the teacher, but the result will be more meaningful thought from the students.

Factual or memory-level questions can eventually lead to higher levels of questions and thinking. A student must first be familiar with the basics in order to reach the level required to answer a higher-level question. For example, to answer the complex question "What is the relationship between the depth and pressure of water?" the teacher and student must know some basic facts about water and pressure.

Benjamin Bloom (1971), an early writer on levels of thinking, called the basic level "knowledge." He discovered that, when students are asked to make up questions on a topic, most of their questions are lower-level. The teacher's leadership is required to help students think beyond this minimum level.

Bloom's hierarchy of question levels is as follows:

Higher Level: 1. Evaluation
2. Synthesis
3. Analysis
4. Application
5. Comprehension
    (a) Translation
    (b) Interpretation
    (c) Inference
Lower Level: 6. "Knowledge"/Memory/Fact

These levels are elaborated in Figure 10.1.

Figure 10.1

BLOOM'S LEVELS OF QUESTIONS TO GUIDE THINKING

Level	Guide Words	Example
1. Evaluation judgment based on criterion	judge, criticize, evaluate, justify	What are the advantages and disadvantages of computers? Should the police pay criminals for information? Who should get the bounce balls first?
2. Synthesis putting together parts to create a new whole	combine, develop, formulate, create, invent, hypothesize, improve	How could you create a new animal from junkyard pieces? What hypothesis could explain the results of the experiment? How could you organize the gym team to form a peace symbol?
3. Analysis breaking down the whole	categorize, dissect, compare, subdivide	Can you categorize the words in the sentence into parts of speech?
4. Application apply the known to a new situation	model, construct, apply, demonstrate	If the volume of the cyclinder had exploded earlier, what might have happened? Can you draw a diagram to show how plant seeds are transported? Can you predict the price of wheat if there is a crop failure?
5. Comprehension (a) translation explain in your own words	restate, show, paraphrase	What was meant by the man's firm handshake? What does the phrase mean?
(b) interpretation find the relationships among ideas	relate, explain	What does the graph mean? Which picture illustrates the meaning of the story?
(c) inference connect ideas from known to unknown	interpret	What might the sailors have traded for the parrot? What season of the year does it appear to be? What would have happened if he had chosen a different casket?

6. Knowledge		
memory and recall of basic facts	what, why, where, how many, remember	Who is the Prime Minister?
		When did the Inuit boy go hunting?
		Where do we place the decimal?

It is important to realize that there is not universal agreement in categorizing the various levels of questions. Some questions could be categorized in more than one level, depending on the context in which they were asked. For example, "Why did the people move?" could be an interpretation question because the student would have to explain various reasons for people moving. On the other hand, if the answer to the question was given the previous day, this question would be a memory-level question.

Identifying the precise level of a question is less important than adhering to the principle of asking a variety of questions, and asking higher-level questions to stretch students' thinking beyond the minimal knowledge/fact/memory level.

These levels apply to longer assignments as well as to oral or written questions answered in class. More time must be allowed to enable students to respond to questions and assignments which require higher levels of thinking.

SKILLS FOR QUESTIONING

Clarifying Teacher Questions

To ensure that students do not have difficulty understanding teacher questions, use the following techniques for effective questioning.

1. Make the question stand apart from other talk by (a) bracketing the question with silence and (b) changing the inflection in your voice.
2. Make your questions as clear as possible. (a) Limit yourself to a single question. Avoid multiple questions such as "Where and when did the apple fall off the tree?" (b) Avoid interrupting your own question with additional information halfway through the question. An example of a fragmented or interrupted question would be "What is the annual rainfall . . . remember from yesterday . . . of the Great Plains in summer?" (c) Avoid rhetorical questions, in which you supply the answer yourself, as in "Where is the subject in this sentence? It's right at the start, isn't it?"

    Gauge the clarity of your own questions by students' looks of confusion or requests for further explanation. Help your students to understand. Write your questions out beforehand. The written questions may reveal your lack of verbal clarity.

3. Avoid run-on questions. These happen when a teacher attempts to ask a question, realizes that the question has not been understood, and tries to rephrase it again and again. For example: "What were the motives of the man who froze to death? What was driving him? Why did he go to the farm? Why did he go there when he wasn't interested in his friend's wife? Or was he?"

Questioning for Student Involvement

To ensure that your questions engage the greatest number students consider the following pointers.

1. Distribute questions equitably throughout your class so that all students get involved.
2. Ask both volunteers and non-volunteers for answers to your questions.
3. Avoid asking questions in a recognizable pattern, such as up and down rows or alphabetically by student names. Some students will stop participating if they can anticipate that they won't be called on.
4. Classroom management difficulties sometimes emerge with "chorus" answers or "call-outs." It may, however, be appropriate at times to encourage group responses, as some students feel inhibited when singled out. You may want to direct some questions to individuals and some to the class as a whole. Group response to simple yes or no questions can be indicated with thumbs up for yes and thumbs down for no. Some teachers have students touch their lips for yes and their chin for no. Cards with two colours on opposite sides could also be used. All of these "whole class" responses ensure that *all* students are held accountable, although such procedures should not be overdone.
5. Avoid repeating your questions. You want to encourage students to pay close attention. (Exceptions might need to be made in some oral language drills and when students have hearing or language difficulties.)
6. Avoid giving a clue before students have a chance to answer the question. For example: "Which king granted the charter to the Hudson's Bay Company? Which Charles did that?"
7. Have backup questions ready to challenge students of different ability, learning styles, or interests. Be prepared to rephrase a question if it needs reiteration from another point of view.
8. Group the class into pairs and let the partners take turns asking

and answering questions. Peer questioning allows students to formulate questions and answers and to participate in a non-threatening one-to-one relationship.

9. Formulate questions at a variety of levels of difficulty. Distribute the questions according to students' ability so that as many students as possible can achieve success.

10. Consider the background of your students to avoid offending them with your questions. Teachers must be sensitive to the economic, political, social, ethnic, and religious realities in their classrooms.

11. Formulate questions at various thinking levels, preferably in a pattern that culminates in a higher-level assignment, project, or final oral question.

RESPONDING TO STUDENTS

The way in which a teacher responds to students affects their subsequent behaviour and thinking. Let's consider several ways that teachers might respond to students.

WAIT-TIME

A common concern of beginning teachers is "What if I ask a question and get no response from my students?" This is not unusual, and it is certainly no reason for a teacher to panic. Instead of rushing to fill the silence, just wait and see what happens.

An appropriate wait-time is usually three to five seconds. After a teacher asks a question and waits an appropriate length of time, a student may volunteer a response or the teacher may ask a particular student to respond. This may be followed by a further wait before the student elaborates on his or her initial response or another student volunteers.

Teachers tend to not allow sufficient wait time because they feel uncomfortable in periods of extended silence. With experience and confidence, teachers can learn to utilize teacher silence very effectively.

Wait-time encourages all students to think about and respond to a question. Both the quantity and the quality of student responses will increase if wait-time is given. For this reason, it is usually more effective to ask the question before asking a particular student to respond. For example: "In what ways might the building of a pipeline effect the arctic eco-system we have been talking about? [Wait-time of three seconds.] Raji?" This is referred to as the "directed questioning" technique. Figure 10.2 illustrates a cycle of teacher questioning, wait-time, and student response.

FIGURE 10.2
WAIT-TIME

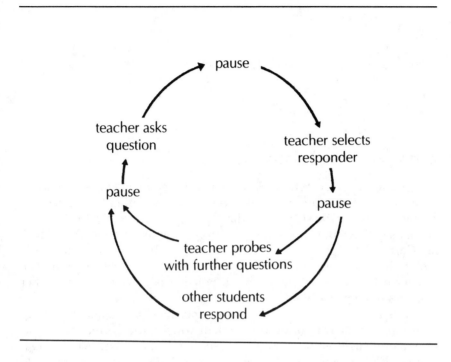

PRAISE AND ENCOURAGEMENT

Positive response from the teacher encourages further participation by students during class discussions. Students lacking self-confidence need positive feedback, and more confident students often demand it because they are accustomed to receiving it.

Accentuate the positive. Rather than marking an X beside the few incorrect items on a student's assignment, put check marks beside every correct answer. Then the student would see all the positive check marks rather than the glaring X-marks for the few errors that were made. Display student work. Students respond more positively in a room that displays their work and interests.

The use of body language can be very effective. Smiling, nodding one's head, raising one's eyebrows, or opening one's arms wide sends a message of acceptance to students. A teacher's positive attitude is an inspiring and powerful force for learning and for developing a positive classroom climate.

Choice of words is important in communicating praise and reinforcement. The following expressions will send students positive messages.

Thank you very much.
Wow!
Keep it up.
You really outdid yourself today.
You're on the right track now.
Good thinking.
You are very good at that.

ALTERNATIVE WAYS TO SAY "NO"

The teacher must let students know whether their responses are correct or incorrect. Don't ignore incorrect responses, or students will become confused. The quickest way for the teacher to communicate this is to simply say "no." But responding to students with a simple "Yes"/"No" or "Correct"/"Incorrect" creates two problems: It encourages guessing, and a flat "no" discourages further thinking and participation. The teacher needs to explain why the response was incorrect, or get other students to help clarify it.

Another technique is to say "no" and then ask some follow-up questions which will guide the student toward the correct response. Comments such as "Let's think about this some more. What would happen if we crossed out the number here? What do we need to do to the other part of the equation? What do we have to know about the rule for these equations?" can re-orient students. An alternative is to ask other students to offer an explanation or point of view: "What do you think of Petri's statement?" "What evidence supports what Tara just said?" "Could there be another reason?" "What might Bob have been thinking of when he said that?"

Occasionally, it is appropriate to let students know that you do not know the answer. A teacher might say, for example, "I"m not sure. Does anyone have any ideas?" This encourages students to provide responses. Experience and confidence enables a teacher to lead students to further responses by occasionally using this technique.

PARAPHRASES AND PERCEPTION CHECKS

When a student makes a comment, the teacher can check the student's meaning by asking "Did you mean that . . .?" or "Are you saying that . . .?" It is important that the student's comments be reworded in the form of a question, in case the teacher has misinterpreted what the student said. It's presumptuous to say (rather than ask) "What you really mean is. . . ."

Perception checks occur when the teacher recognizes displays of students' feelings and responds to them. Students may feel confused, be proud of their accomplishments, or be struck by something funny. A teacher may see a tear roll down a child's cheek and say "What's wrong?" or notice a student's big smile and say "You like that humour!"

NON-VERBAL RESPONSES

Smiles, nods, frowns, and puzzled looks can be as meaningful as words. Eye contact with students often is important, although teachers need to be aware that this is less acceptable in some cultures. Leaning toward students can indicate interest or concern. Moving near students and walking up and down the aisles between desks or across the room can increase students' awareness of the teacher.

NEGATIVE RESPONSES

Negative responses such as sarcasm and belittling students must be avoided. If a teacher picks on students, one of two things usually occurs: the class resents the teacher or, even worse, other students start picking on the student who has been singled out by the teacher.

When a teacher has to resort to rude remarks or slang, it is time to consider another career. Expressions such as "shut up," "drop dead," "who cares," "grow up," or "you are a jerk" are inexcusable. Respect for students must be shown by being polite, friendly, and interested in them.

KNOWING THE INTENT OF YOUR RESPONSES

A teacher's responses do not necessarily convey the same message to everyone in the classroom. For example, if a teacher responds to a student's comment by saying "good," "yes," or "you're correct," we assume that these positive responses will make students more apt to speak out during a class discussion.

In fact, the opposite may be true! Although the student who made the comment may be encouraged, such statements can discourage further group discussion by suggesting that the one correct answer has already been given. Another student, particularly if quieter or less confident, may have thought of another valid response to the question, but be inhibited from responding.

Assume you have a class in which most students are quiet and withdrawn. You want to encourage more class discussion. If one of the students makes a comment, your response could either inhibit other students from participating or make them feel free to discuss the ideas further. Are the responses in the following list likely to be freeing or inhibiting for this type of class?

1. "Stand and speak in complete sentences."
2. "How do you feel?"
3. "I know you don't mean that."
4. "Everyone doesn't have to agree."
5. "How many agree with that? Raise your hands."
6. "I won't answer any questions during this discussion."
7. "We don't use such words here."
8. "Now, let's discuss that point for a few minutes."
9. "How does this relate to what we were discussing yesterday?"
10. "It's alright to say what you feel."
11. "Raise your hand and wait to be called on."
12. "Let him finish his thought."
13. "Can you prove that?"
14. "What do you think?"
15. "Look that up in the reference book I gave you."

The even-numbered responses are non-judgmental and encourage more discussion, particularly with students not usually inclined to respond in class. The odd-numbered responses are judgmental and tend to inhibit further discussion.

At some point, of course, the teacher will *want* to end the discussion. The point of this exercise is that teachers should be aware of the effects that their responses have on students.

ANALYZING CLASSROOM INTERACTIONS

Read Interaction 10-1, or act it out with your peers. Analyze the questions asked in it. Note the indefinite and multiple questions asked at the beginning. Find some multiple and interrupted questions. Where is the teacher's rhetorical question? Note how the teacher repeated many students' comments. What might be the effect of doing this?

INTERACTION 10-1: A LESSON ON POPULATION

Teacher: When we talked about all of those different places, all . . . er . . . each of them had different sizes or different numbers of people in them. *When we talk about populations, what do we mean?* If we are talking about towns or cities or farms, what does the word "population" mean? Jonathan.

Jonathan: I guess it means how many people there are.

Teacher: *Right.* Mm-hmm. How many people . . . So is the population . . . *Where is the largest population?* Emily.

Emily: In one of the big cities.

Teacher: *OK.* Would it be . . . *Would the population be bigger in Calgary or in Toronto?* It would be Toronto, right? *Where would the population be smallest?* (All students respond.) Hands up, please. Mike.

Mike: In the North.

Teacher: OK. So that means there is only one person per large area or one family. There would be one family, and there would be a lot of area. *Right. So what are some animals that are grouped into populations?* Kevin.

Kevin: Gophers.

Teacher: Prairie dogs. *What is another one?* Paul?

Paul: Lemmings.

Teacher: Mm-hmm. Right. Amber?

Amber: Caribou.

Teacher: Yes. Ricky?

Ricky: Dogs, cats, horses, sheep, rats, mice. All farm animals.

Teacher: Right. So we have a lot of different animals that we've grouped into populations. *What are some of those populations called?* Crystal?

Crystal: Towns — prairie dog towns.

Teacher: Right. Jennifer?

Jennifer: Schools.

Teacher: Right, that's with fish.

Liam: Packs of wolves.

Teacher: Packs. Kirsten.

Kirsten: Flocks.

Teacher: Right, *and what are grouped into colonies?*

Robin: Bees.

Teacher: Bees. Any other animals or anything else? Let's look at the filmstrip now.

What levels and types of questions were asked by the teacher in Interaction 10-1? Can you detect any pattern of questioning? Did the teacher, through a questioning pattern, lead the students to some important conclusions about the topic?

Now read or role-play Interaction 10-2. Look at the variety of responses used by this teacher. How would you feel if you were a student with a teacher who responded in this manner?

INTERACTION 10-2: A LESSON ON NUTRITION

Teacher: Please take out your Canada Food Guide. What food groups would Jamie's breakfast include? Brady.

Brady: Cereal would cover one serving in the breads and cereals category.

Teacher: Good! What else does Jamie's breakfast cover? Darren.

Darren: A serving of milk products would be covered by the milk with the cereal.

Teacher: Great! Good thinking, Darren. What would yogurt fit into? Aden.

Aden: The milk group also.

Teacher: Super. Praha, would you tell us what you had for breakfast?

Praha: Toast.

Teacher: What type of bread did you have?

Praha: White bread.

Teacher: How could Praha have improved the nutritional value of his breakfast? Vince.

Vince: He could have used whole-wheat bread.

Teacher: Good answer, Vince. Why would whole-wheat bread be more nutritious? Blair.

Blair: It has more carbohydrates and fibre.

Teacher: Blair, you're correct! Whole-wheat bread has more fibre. What did the information in the pamphlet tell us? Lindsay?

Lindsay: We should cut down on our fat intake.

Teacher: How many think that fat in our diet is important? Good. What role does fat play in our body functioning? Kim.

Kim: It helps keep us warm.

Teacher: Great! Does anyone have another thought?

Steven: It produces energy.

Teacher: Excellent, fat is a source of energy! Do you see any problems in completely eliminating fats from our diet?

Michelle: We will lack energy and warmth.

Teacher: Now you're thinking. Good! What else do we have to eat more of to keep our bodies going? Carlos.

Carlos: Carbohydrates.

Teacher: Super answer. What else should we eat more of?

Rebecca: Fruits and vegetables.

Teacher: (Makes thumbs-up gesture.) Why?

Diane: They give us vitamins and minerals.

Teacher: Which foods are your favourites?

Jamie: Pizza and burgers.

Mike: Pop and ice-cream.

Chris: Chips, fries and gravy.

Teacher: What would you conclude about the food we like in comparison to the Canada Food Guide?

Tom: We don't like things that are good for us.

Debbie: We need to eat different kinds of food to keep healthy.

Teacher: These are really important points. Wow! We really learned something here!

Chapter Eleven:
CLASSROOM
MANAGEMENT

Main Understandings

In this chapter you will learn the following:

1. No single approach to the complexities of classroom management is sufficient.
2. The behaviour of students can depend on contexts beyond the individual or the classroom.
3. A great deal of classroom management depends on planning, instructional procedures, and rules and regulations.
4. Classroom management requires a range of teacher roles which include modifying behaviour, listening to and counselling students, and seeking outside help.
5. Today's students require classroom management practices which focus on their personal needs and social contexts.
6. Individual accountability and self-actualization are the ultimate goals of classroom management.

Decision-making is the key to classroom management. As illustrated in Figure 11.1, decisions about classroom management are influenced by the teacher's personal beliefs and attitudes, and these in turn are influenced by a variety of factors which are identified in the squares surrounding the centre of the diagram.

FIGURE 11.1
DIMENSIONS OF CLASSROOM MANAGEMENT

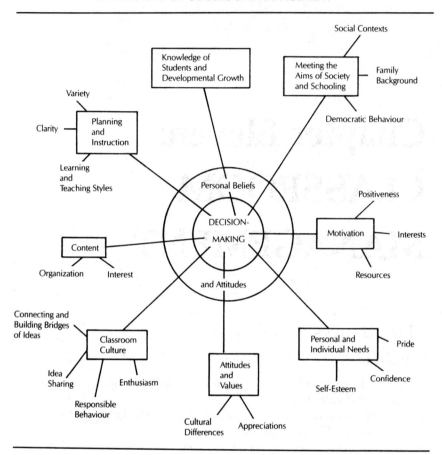

The behaviour of students must also be viewed within a variety of influential contexts. As illustrated in Figure 11.2, student behaviour may be influenced by such factors as personal stresses, interactions with other students, home situation, after-school activities, or television.

FIGURE 11.2
CONTEXTS OF CLASSROOM MANAGEMENT

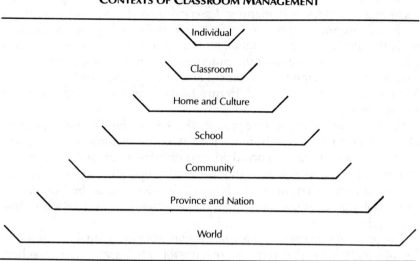

APPROACHES TO CLASSROOM MANAGEMENT

How can a teacher respond to the challenges of classroom management and discipline? Figure 11.3 illustrates a spectrum of approaches. The best approach will vary with each situation, depending on the teacher's objectives, the severity of the discipline problem, and the maturity and the needs of the students.

FIGURE 11.3
A SPECTRUM OF APPROACHES TO CLASSROOM MANAGEMENT

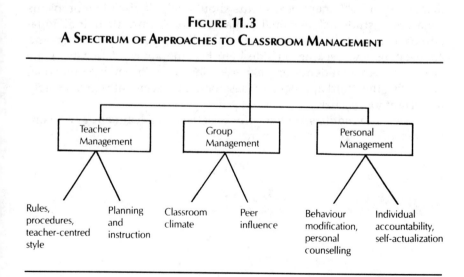

In *teacher-dominated management*, the teacher behaves assertively, communicating rules and procedures to students clearly, firmly, and in a businesslike but friendly manner. Assertiveness should not be confused with aggression: assertive communication is free of threats or displays of bad temper. Teacher-dominated management also relies on good planning and effective teaching practices, which will automatically take care of many discipline problems. Lack of planning usually results in low-quality instruction, which in turn leads to problems with classroom management.

In the *group management* approach, the key is developing a positive classroom climate through democratic decision-making involving students. If students are involved in determining rules and procedures, they will feel more a part of the system for operating their classroom or school rather than mere receivers of decisions made by the teacher or school administrator. Peer influence is a major consideration in this approach.

The *personal management* approach encourages individual accountability. Students learn that they are responsible for their actions. Teachers themselves may act as listeners and counsellors, but when necessary they will seek outside help from school psychologists, the justice system, social workers, special-interest organizations, and medical experts.

Before deciding on an approach to classroom management, the teacher must identify the reason for the discipline problem. If it is the result of a lack of good planning and instruction, then that is the area the teacher will need to work on. If it is due to a group or peer influence, then developing a positive classroom environment and encouraging the democratic involvement of students should help. If discipline problems stem from students' personal behaviour problems, then individual approaches such as behaviour-modification practices, listening and counselling, and seeking outside help become appropriate. Given the fact that many students are experiencing stress from dysfunctional family life, this third approach to classroom management is increasingly important for teachers.

Figure 11.4 identifies keys for the effective establishment and maintenance of classroom management.

FIGURE 11.4
KEYS TO CLASSROOM MANAGEMENT

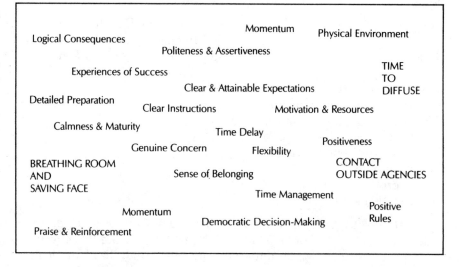

TEACHER MANAGEMENT

There are two aspects to teacher management: (a) rules and procedures and (b) planning and instruction.

RULES AND PROCEDURES

Rules and procedures may be determined entirely by the teacher, but if they are formulated through discussion with students, students usually respond more positively to them.

A few basic positive rules are more effective than negative rules or too many rules. Positive rules express desirable behaviours. Examples are: "Wait your turn so it is fair to others." "Follow the rules of the game so everyone can have more fun." "Respect the property and right of other students so they will do the same for you." Note that these positive rules have two parts. One part expresses the rule and the other part expresses a positive reason for that rule. People are more likely to follow rules if they know the reasons behind them.

In the following examples, provide a reason for the rule as illustrated in the first two items.

Rule	Reason
Walk in single file . . .	to avoid bumping into others in the hall.
Walk, don't run, in the hall . . .	so people don't get knocked down.
Check with the teacher before sharpening your pencil . . .	
Throw your lunch wrappers in the garbage cans . . .	
Be at your desks before the second bell . . .	
Freeze on the gym floor when the whistle blows . . .	

Negative rules express forbidden behaviours. Examples of negative rules are: "Don't run" or "No talking." Negative rules are less effective than positive rules. For example, the negative rule "Don't interrupt someone when they are talking" is better expressed positively as "Let others finish speaking before you talk so they have a chance to finish their thoughts."

Rules and procedures should be stated briefly, simply, and clearly to students. If students follow the rules, give them positive feedback. If they break them, address the inappropriate behaviour promptly and consistently. (Discipline problems usually do not evaporate of their own accord.) Teach rules and procedure at appropriate times. Students are usually not able to internalize a lot of rules or procedures at one time.

Being polite yet assertive is important in classroom management. Say firmly "Please turn on your computers now" rather than asking "Do you want to turn on your computers now?"

Rules and procedures are considered good if they are:

- Brief
- Positive
- Reasonable
- Clearly communicated
- Consistent
- Related clearly to consequences
- Associated with reasons for them

Logical Consequences

Logical consequences are natural outgrowths of behaviour chosen by the students. They teach students to be responsible for their own actions. They also enable teachers to avoid having to continually remind students how to behave.

The teacher must think through the consequences carefully in advance, not react to students' behaviour on the spur of the moment. Logical consequences are not the same as punishment.

For example, a Phys Ed teacher might make a rule that after drill all equipment must be put away, or students will not be allowed a scrimmage during the latter half of Phys Ed class. One consequence is that students will put all the equipment away and there will be a scrimmage; another consequence is that students will not put all the equipment away and there will be no scrimmage. There are no exceptions and no arguments about this rule. Students decide which consequence they wish to choose.

GROUP MANAGEMENT

The peer group is a major influence on student behaviour, and can cause discipline problems in the classroom. Knowledge of peer influence can be acquired through a sociogram which shows student preferences for others in the same class or school. To construct a sociogram, follow these steps:

1. Ask students to write the names of two other students whom they would like to work with on a project, play with, do things with, or sit beside.
2. Tabulate their choices.
3. Draw lines to indicate their choices.

In the sociogram shown in Figure 11.5, Maria is very popular. Phoebe may be isolated from this group of girls. Phoebe, Celine, and Tess prefer to do things with Maria, but Maria's first choice is Shih-Ping. Shih-Ping and Maria appear to be the best of friends. Shih-Ping and Shabnum may be friends, but the first choice of a friend for each of them is someone else. For the other people, reciprocal choices for friends do not exist.

What are the reasons for these preferences? Are they based on academic ability, personality, looks, or clothes? Is the type of home or where someone lives in the community a factor? Is racial or ethnic background a factor? How important is talent or physical ability? Knowing students' interpersonal preferences and the reasons for them helps a teacher understand, accommodate, and influence student behaviour.

Figure 11.5
Sociogram of Student Relationships

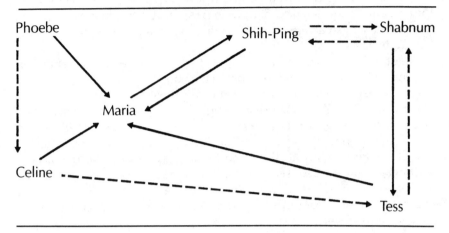

Note: Solid lines represent first choices; broken lines indicate second choices.

MOTIVATION

Motivation is a major factor in classroom management. Once a teacher discovers what students want or are interested in, this information may be used to counteract many classroom management problems. For example, Mr. Rizzo, a math teacher, knew his students liked to get to the gymnasium early to set up the.nets for volleyball and play for a few minutes before other students arrived for house leagues during the noon hour. He would say to his students "Let's get these math exercises completed correctly so we can have some time in the gym before noon." Students were motivated to do their work efficiently and correctly. Mr. Rizzo never used a negative approach ("If you don't finish your work you cannot go to the gym"). Teachers have also used this positive approach with special projects, activity centres, or computers as the incentive.

Praise and reinforcement is important for motivation. Make the praise specific to the situation or task. For example, rather than simply saying "Good," it is more effective to say "The assignment was very well done because it was neatly written and all parts were completed."

Managing group work requires following clear procedures. Avoid long student presentations. Be aware of activities being carried out by other groups while you work with one group or with an individual student.

Create a classroom environment in which students feel free to ask questions and express their views. Focus on the positive characteristics of students. "Catch them being good" and build on that success.

Ensure success in learning and completing assignments so that students feel good about themselves and their classroom. Don't tolerate domination by an individual student or an in-group within the class. Never belittle or use sarcasm. Project an image of tolerance, patience, and fairness. Encourage students to ask questions and inquire about ideas, rather than acting as if you know all the answers. Share the power of decision-making with your students. They will feel the excitement of learning if their teacher projects a sense of inquisitiveness and exploration.

One technique for developing a democratic climate is to conduct classroom meetings. Topics for discussion might be found in the curriculum, a community issue such as drug abuse, or school issues such as playground regulations or organizing class parties or dances.

Arrange students in a circle with no books, pens, or papers to interfere with the meeting. The rules are:

1. Anyone may talk.
2. You don't have to talk if you don't feel like it.
3. There are no "right" or "wrong" things to say.
4. There are no follow-up assignments.

The teacher acts as a group facilitator. She or he does not ask specific questions of individual students, but rather encourages everyone to respond to open-ended questions addressed to the entire group. These questions should not be asked in a predetermined sequence, but should arise from the discussion. Respond positively and encourage student comments by avoiding judgments about what students have said.

Classroom meetings build students' problem-solving skills. Opportunities to participate in the group decision-making process build positive feelings. Successful classroom meetings create more positive attitudes and behaviour in students. Once classroom meetings have been established they can become an excellent way of airing class concerns related to matters of discipline.

Personal Management

Personal management focuses on the individual student. There are procedures which help avoid escalation of common class disruptions by individuals. Non-verbal signals such as a glance, a nod of the head, moving close to a student, or quietly removing an object from a student's hand are ways of deflecting unwanted behaviour. It is important to avoid public confrontation. Take the student aside later and talk with him or her privately.

Sometimes teachers must also contend with more acute problems of personal stress and extreme behaviour. These student behaviours frequently are due to dysfunctional families and/or poverty, which in turn lead to hunger, insecurity, loneliness, anger, lack of routine, and lack of discipline. Alcoholism and drug abuse may play a major role. Other underlying causes may be physical or mental in nature, requiring co-operation with medical, social, and psychological professionals from outside the school.

Some argue that such concerns are beyond the role of the teacher. But these students are in our classrooms, and they affect the behaviours and attitudes of others. The fact that they may not be currently able to function normally in a social and educational environment does not mean they can be denied the benefits of the educational process. They have a right to education and a right to receive help, and at this time in their lives, the school plays a major helping role. Students with extreme learning and behavioural disabilities may be homogeneously grouped into separate classrooms and programs for special attention or they may be "mainstreamed" in with the rest of the student body to experience the modelling of "normal" behaviour.

The role of the teacher in personal management can be to (a) modify behaviour, (b) listen to and counsel students, and (c) seek help outside the school when necessary.

FIGURE 11.6
THREE ROLES OF THE TEACHER IN PERSONAL MANAGEMENT

| to modify behaviour | to listen and counsel | to seek outside help |

BEHAVIOUR MODIFICATION

Behaviour modification is an approach to education in which teachers attempt to alter students' actions or encourage student progress toward positive behavioural or educational goals. Teachers may plan, practise, and adjust their teaching to assist students in behaviour change. Teachers progress through four phases to implement the desired behaviour change: (1) baseline, (2) treatment, (3) reversal, and (4) reintervention.

Figure 11.7 illustrates the example of a teacher who wants to change the behaviour of a student who speaks out in class at inappropriate times.

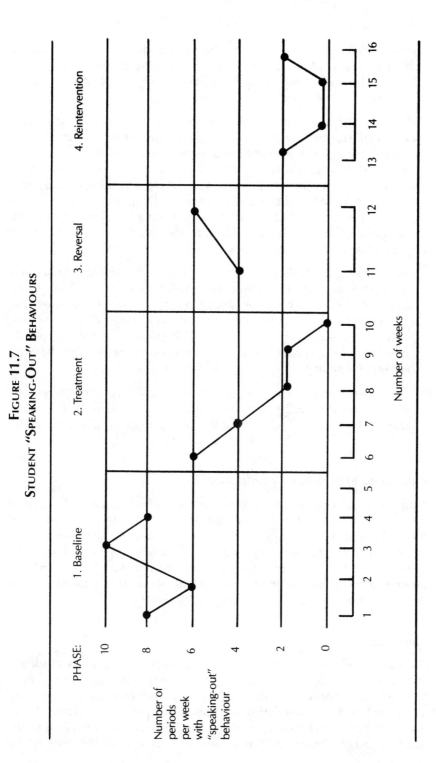

FIGURE 11.7
STUDENT "SPEAKING-OUT" BEHAVIOURS

Phase 1: Chart Baseline Behaviour. The teacher documents the number of times the student spoke out of turn during a 40-minute period. Note that there is a high frequency of speaking-out behaviours at the baseline measure.

Phase 2: Treatment. The teacher reinforces positive behaviour with praise or special treatment and ignores the speaking-out behaviours.

Some examples of positive reinforcers would be placing a student's name on an honour roll, special visits to other classes, or extra time on the class computer. Note in the second column of Figure 11.7, how the treatment reduced the frequency of speaking-out behaviours.

The treatment phase must be carried out over time so that the change in behaviours is internalized by the student. Typical treatment phases last at least three or four weeks.

Phase 3: Reversal. The teacher stops reinforcing the positive behaviour to see if the negative behaviour returns. Teachers often feel uncertain about this return to baseline conditions. At this stage you hope that the positive behaviour has been internalized and that the negative behaviour will not return. In Figure 11.7, during the reversal phase, some increase in speaking-out behaviours occurred, but less than the baseline frequency.

Phase 4: Reintervention. If the negative behaviour still persists, the teacher reintroduces the positive reinforcement or adds a new aspect to the treatment. Figure 11.7 shows that during the reintervention phase the speaking-out behaviours were nearly eliminated.

Limitations of Behaviour Modification

Many teachers hesitate to use behaviour modification on philosophical grounds as it moves the focus of control from the student to external forces. Like all other strategies it may be useful for some students who do not respond to other approaches. Such an approach has merit provided that the external forces (rewards) are withdrawn and the student behaviours remain at an acceptable level. At this point, control of the behaviour should be internalized by the student.

Contracts

Two kinds of contracts may be used by teachers to modify students' behaviour: contingency contracts, student contracts, and action plans.

In a *contingency contract*, the teacher and student usually set a long-term goal such as completing all homework between October 1 and December 20. Short-term rewards or contingencies are provided to the student at timed intervals throughout the duration of the plan. In the sample contract shown in Figure 11.8, after every two weeks of successfully completing all homework the student is given some privilege or reward.

A *student contract* is an agreement between a teacher and a student to do certain things or behave in certain ways. Unlike contingency contracts, student contracts are not based on a reward structure.

All contracts should be written in a positive manner, stating the desired performance or behaviour. All terms in the contract should be attainable by the student. They should specifically identify the task to be performed and the behaviour to be changed. Contracts are much more effective when they are negotiated with the student rather than imposed on him or her. Consequences of breaking the contract should be agreed on in advance. It is inadvisable to change the terms of the contract in midstream.

FIGURE 11.8
SAMPLE CONTINGENCY CONTRACT

I agree to do the following:
    1. Complete my homework from Monday to Thursday.
    2. Let others decide who takes the ball equipment outside.
If I do this each week I may:
    1. Participate in extracurricular activities and
    2. Eat lunch with my friends.
If I do not do these things each week I agree to:
    1. Stay away from the ball field during breaks.
    2. Eat lunch at my desk.

Date started _____Student _____
Date completed _____Teacher _____

The simplest form of contract is an action plan (see Figure 11.9). This plan is completed by the student and co-signed by the teacher.

FIGURE 11.9
SAMPLE ACTION PLAN

I agree to: _____
Next time I: _____
Teacher _____Date started _____
Student _____Date completed _____

Many of the guidelines for teacher-directed instruction discussed earlier are based on behaviour modification principles of reinforcement, rewards, and praise. These approaches provide students with a choice of computer time, working on a project with another student, stars and stickers, earning points for doing work, etc. Contingency contracts and structured-success classrooms characterized by time-outs, parent cooperation, and strict guidelines use behaviour modification principles for students with more severe behaviour problems.

The emphasis is on describing present behaviour rather than attempting to determine a rationale for that behaviour. The negative approach of taking away rewards or incentives through detention, writing "lines," sitting in the hall, or being expelled from the classroom or school are negative approaches. Negative approaches tend to decrease internalization of students' responsibility for their behaviour and may increase behavioural problems.

THE TEACHER AS LISTENER AND COUNSELLOR

Personal problems of students can be best addressed by teachers who are good listeners. Good teaching and effective classroom management cannot always be achieved by lecturing or organizing students. At times teachers must play a counselling role. Even though the teacher may ask some questions to help the student work out his or her problem, the main role of the teacher is that of a listener, giving the student time to think through and work out the problem. There are three approaches to listening to students: critical listening, sympathetic listening, and creative listening.

CRITICAL LISTENING

The critical listener helps a student separate fact from fiction in order to clearly define the central issue in the problem. It is also essential to help students sort out thoughts based on emotion from thoughts based on reason, and to separate words from actions, and people from their words.

Critical listening questions could begin with "How?" "Why?" or "How true . . .?"

SYMPATHETIC LISTENING

Listen — don't tell. Let the student talk out the problem instead of throwing in your judgments, advice, or conclusions.

Sympathetic listening can be very effective, but it is the least-used form of listening by teachers. It requires skill and self-discipline. Students desperately need a sympathetic ear at times. You don't always have to provide all the answers. The teacher may be the only adult with whom a student gets to talk. Parents may not have the time or the skills to communicate with their children.

CREATIVE LISTENING

Creative listening involves looking for the most useful part of the student's idea, then taking that part and building on it. Working with another person to build new ideas is a rewarding experience for both parties. Students can have good ideas to offer. Treat them with respect.

SKILLS OF A GOOD LISTENER

Every teacher needs to practise the following skills in order to become a good listener.

1. *Control by eye contact*
   Eye contact is necessary both when listening to an individual student and in a group or classroom situation. Glancing out the window, at your wristwatch, or at other people should be avoided. Remember, though, that eye contact may be a cultural taboo for some students.

2. *Effective use of thinking speed*
   A listener is capable of thinking faster than the other person is talking. As the other person speaks, use this time advantage to remind yourself of the important points she or he is making. Ask yourself questions about what the other person is saying. In this way the listener is using thinking speed to advantage.

3. *Avoid too much talk*
   A person cannot listen and talk at the same time. View yourself as an observer. Listen first — then evaluate. Let the other person do most of the talking.

4. *Listen with an open mind*
   Wait to hear an idea from the other person's words that you can use. Don't jump to conclusions.

5. *Separate the words from the speaker*
   Listen for the ideas or meaning behind the words. If you have a prejudicial attitude toward the speaker, it is very difficult to hear what that person is saying. It is important to recognize our prejudices toward a speaker in terms of religion, age, clothing, hairstyle, race, ethnicity, or socioeconomic status and try to overcome them.

6. *Allow time for the speaker*

   Hear others out. Be patient and courteous. Show interest and a willingness to take the time to listen.

7. *Use the basic communication skills*

   Clear communication is essential. The following are four communication skills to practise when working with others.

   - *Paraphrase* the other's comments to make sure you understand them as they were intended. Check to make sure the other person understands your comments in the way you intended them. Repeat in your own words what you heard them say.

   - Use *perception-checking* responses to ensure that you are not making false assumptions about the other's feelings: "I thought you weren't interested in trying to understand my idea. Was I wrong?" "Did my last statement bother you?"

   - *Behaviour descriptions* report the specific acts of the other person: "You cut in before he finished his sentence." "You hit him at the door." At this point, no judgment is made. Your comments are limited to describing the actual behaviour. Judgment and discussions about subsequent actions will occur a little later.

   - *Describe* your *feelings* or ask the student to describe hers or his: "I like what you just said." Describe your feelings in such a way that they are seen as temporary and capable of change rather than as permanent attitudes: "Right now I'm very annoyed with you." The least helpful statements are those that sound as if they are information about the other person but are really expressions of your own feelings. Such statements push a student into a defensive position. Some examples are: *judgments* about the other person ("You never pay any attention"), *name-calling* and *trait-labelling* ("You're a phony" "You're too rude"), *accusing* the other of undesirable motives ("You enjoy putting people down" "You always have to be the centre of attention"), *commands* and orders ("Stop laughing" "Don't talk so much"), and *sarcasm*.

   "I" statements are more effective for classroom management. Say "I would like it if you stayed in line" rather than "You should stay in line." "You" statements often sound negative and accusing: "You are out of line." Statements which use absolutes are even more negative: "You *never* stay in line" or "You are *always* standing out of line."

   In contrast, "I" statements result in better classroom management. Statements should be tentative in tone as in "I would like it if you showed more concern for other students" rather than an absolute statement such as "You don't care for others and you never will."

   Statements are more helpful if they are . . .

   - specific rather than general: "You bumped my cup" rather than "You never watch where you're going."

- tentative rather than absolute: "You seem unconcerned about Jimmy" rather than "You couldn't care less about Jimmy and never will."
- informing rather than ordering: "I hadn't finished yet" rather than "Stop interrupting me."

SEEKING OUTSIDE HELP

Classroom management should be a team effort. When a school staff works together, classroom management is less of a challenge. School administrators and teachers set the tone for the whole school — in the hallways, on the school grounds, in the gym — as well as inside every classroom. Talk to other teachers and the school administration.

Teachers are sometimes required to seek assistance from agencies outside the school. Court workers, social workers, and the police can play an essential role in helping some students work through difficult behaviour problems. Psychological testing and medical evaluations provide information needed to help students, and these resources are channelled through the school.

In 1987 Statistics Canada defined 17 percent of children under 17 in Canada as "poor." More than 150,000 Canadian children are regular users of food banks. Many students in poverty run an increased risk of physical, social, and emotional problems. Malnutrition, absenteeism, neglect and abuse, transience, inappropriate clothing, behaviour problems, low motivation, low achievement, and low self-esteem often characterize children in poverty. Poverty drags them down and deprives them of their right to a happy and healthy life.

First, teachers must determine the causes of behaviour problems. Students of low-income families may have little choice in the way they look or behave, but can be highly intelligent and capable. It is important not to prejudge these students. Second, use support programs that are available in many schools.

LEARNING DISABILITIES AND BEHAVIOUR PROBLEMS

In this section we will look at three types of behavioural disorders: attention-deficit hyperactivity disorder (ADHD), alcohol or drug abuse, and child abuse.

ATTENTION-DEFICIT HYPERACTIVITY DISORDER (ADHD)

Learning disabilities, neurological disorders, and depression may be associated with ADHD. Children with ADHD have also been referred to by other labels such as "the attention-deficit learner" and "the impossible child." This disorder is very complex, but may be identified by the following characteristics in the student:

- Forgetfulness.
- Short attention span. Easily distracted. Rushes from activity to activity.
- Unable to organize schoolwork, bedroom, clothes, etc.
- Fails to complete work.
- Easily locked into obsessions to compensate for distractability.
- Hyperactive. High energy. Always on the go and into everything. Easily bored and continually seeking something new. Fidgets or paces the floor.
- Inappropriate dress — e.g., boots with shorts, long black gowns, over-sized clothes.
- Accident-prone.
- Impulsive. Acts without thought or reason. Poor planning. Lack of sound judgment.
- Inconsistent sleep patterns.
- Outspoken.
- Egocentric. "Me-first" mentality. "Can dish it out but can't take it".
- Insensitive.
- Subject to mood swings. Short-tempered.
- Inclined to tell "white lies." When asked why, they tell things near the truth but not quite the truth.
- Erratic eating patterns.

Many students may have some of these characteristics, so beware: Generalizations can be misleading. Each situation and person is unique and there are varying degrees of disabilities.

The fields of education and medicine are, however, gaining knowledge in dealing with students of special learning and behavioural disabilities. Evidence suggests that these types of behaviour may occur because of malfunctions in the neurotransmitters which send messages between specialized lobes in the brain. These tissues may be weak and a hit-or-miss passage of messages occurs. In some cases, stimulants have produced a more efficient neurotransmitter pattern, thereby moderating the student's behaviour.

What are some ways to help the learning-disabled student? For many who exhibit the characteristics of ADHD, the usual behaviour-manage-ment techniques are not effective. These youngsters can be extremely resistant to "normal" discipline. They often drop out of school, or are expelled, if their behaviour problems cannot be controlled. They are the potential drifters and street people of the future. Sometimes their behaviour can be influenced only through making deals: "Do this, and I'll take you there," or "I'll buy you that." Such behaviour may persist into adulthood.

Successful intervention may come only though medication. Although medical tests cannot determine conclusively the extent to which a student has ADHD, medication under a doctor's care has helped many people suffering from this disorder. The Mental Health Committee of the Canadian Paediatric Society has recommended drug therapy for children and adolescents suffering from ADHD.

Some evidence appears to support the use of medication when extreme behaviours are genetically caused. This is in contrast to those learning disabilities caused through brain-tissue destruction. Examples of these latter disabilities include head injuries, fetal alcohol syndrome, Rhys syndrome, iron deficiency, encephalitis, or lead poisoning.

Teachers need to sort through the information in this new area of classroom management which is placing greater stress and demands on schools. Opinions are varied on drug use *under medical supervision* for managing behaviour. Are the medications addictive? Is there evidence that some behaviours can be brought to near-normality with drug use? What are the side effects? What behaviours occur when the medication is reduced or terminated? What are the *alternatives* to drug therapy to assist in counteracting negative and potentially destructive behaviour? Issues being explored in medicine are having repercussions in the schools of today.

DRUG ABUSE

Drug abuse has risen in our society to the point where most classrooms will have students affected by some form of drug abuse. Drug abuse is considered to be a family disease because it affects all members of the drug user's family emotionally and/or physically. Alcohol is the most commonly used drug among young people, although there are many others such as inhalants (glue, paint thinners, nail polish, gasoline, lighter fluid, and aerosol sprays), marijuana, hallucinogens, cocaine, tranquilizers, barbiturates (depressants), amphetamines (stimulants), and opiates (opium, heroin, and morphine). Canadian statistics indicate that in the early 1990s the leading cause of death among 16-to-19-year-olds is traffic accidents, half of which involve a drinking driver. Nearly half of all drivers killed on Canadian roads were legally impaired at the times of their accidents.

Schools need to see drug abuse not as a moral issue but as a social problem. In schools we tend to treat the symptoms, such as tiredness and absence, but fail to deal with the drug problem itself. For many youngsters, the school is the only ray of hope in lives surrounded by drug abuse. Today's students live in a society which has a drug mentality. For example, it is acceptable to take pills to go to sleep, to stay up long hours and study, etc. Value shifts have occurred in society regarding the ethics of smoking, sex, and work, to name only a few examples.

For many students, school is the most stable factor in their lives.

The Role of the Teacher

Teachers can play three roles in helping youngsters combat drug abuse: (a) impart knowledge, (b) diagnose and report suspected drug abuse, and (c) initiate intervention programs.

A teacher needs to become aware and informed with respect to drug abuse, and to avoid using scare tactics with students. Government agencies and special-interest groups provide information and counselling services on various forms of drugs and their abuse. This information is designed for students at both the elementary and secondary levels, and should be shared with them.

Some of the symptoms of drug abuse are a sudden drop or gradual lowering in grades, skipping classes, dropping out of sports or extra-curricular activities, disrespect and defiance, inattentiveness, sleepiness, wandering aimlessly, frequent trips to the bathroom, excessive use of the telephone, writing slang and phrases regarding drugs on books, and a lack of response to concern expressed by teachers. Students who are abusing drugs may experience sudden changes in emotional state, weight changes, and slurred speech patterns. Reporting these and other symptoms of drug abuse is the first step in an intervention program. To turn your head and look the other way while students flounder is irresponsible.

The following procedures can be followed in an intervention program designed to help students suffering from drug abuse.

1. Prepare for the intervention interview. Speak to other staff members and anyone else who might have information about the student's behaviour. Sort out fact from opinion. For example, "I think there is something wrong with that student" is an opinion; "He has a glazed look" is a fact. Attempt to separate information that pertains directly to potential drug abuse from information regarding other kinds of behavioural changes. Decide on which information you will use at the meeting. Be prepared to refer to written information. Finally, mentally prepare the sequence of the meeting or role play the entire session with another person.
2. Schedule a meeting with the student and parent(s) or guardian(s). You might decide to meet with the student alone initially. If so, the meeting with parents or guardians must follow soon after. Expect denial on the part of the student and parent(s) or guardian(s) at first. It is difficult to admit that one's child has a drug problem, because it implies failure in parenting. Parents and guardians need help to overcome this typical reaction.

Denial may take several forms: (1) "The problem is not all that bad. It is a common thing for young people to do." (2) "The teacher and/or society is to blame." (3) "We can't seem to remember anything about that." (4) "Other kids are at fault, not our own."

Remember that it often takes a crisis to break down the wall of denial. This crisis may occur in the form of an arrest, getting kicked out of school, or being called into a meeting with the teacher.

Four elements need to be present for this important meeting with parents or guardians.

(a) Hold the meeting on your turf. Meet at the school, preferably in your own classroom where you are most comfortable.

(b) Outnumber the parent(s) or guardian(s) at the meeting by having other teachers and staff members present for support.

(c) Allow adequate time for the meeting. It often takes an hour to an hour and a half for the emotional process to evolve during this meeting. Over this time, parent(s) or guardian(s) begin to see and hear what you are saying. They may have heard it before but have refused to acknowledge it. During the meeting you are really inviting them into your thinking process. You have told them that you care about their child. As a result some common ground between you and the parent(s) or guardian(s) can be established.

(d) Have information on the nature of the drug problem available. Be able to tell them where resources are located and what they can do to counteract the problem.

Organize the emotional process which evolves during the meeting into two parts. The first part deals with the symptoms of the drug abuse only. At some point the dramatic moment arrives in which you say the word "drugs." The parent(s) or guardian(s) may respond with anger, but remember that anger is a common cover-up when we are scared. You are the bearer of bad news, so anger can be turned on you. Be prepared to absorb this anger until the parent(s) or guardian(s) work it out. They will come to understand that they are not really angry at you but at the situation. Respond by saying "I'm angry too." Ride with the emotional flow and you will reach the point at which the parent(s) or guardian(s) will ask "What can we do?" When that happens, everyone is on the same side.

The first intervention meeting may not be a complete success. The parent(s) or guardian(s) may need another crisis before they can break down the walls of denial. They may walk out of the meeting, but they will probably return when a further crisis occurs and they reach the point of accepting your offer of help. They will return to you because you had the courage to say "I care and I'm prepared to help do something about it."

CHILD ABUSE

Child abuse occurs when children suffer serious physical injury, neglect, malnutrition, and sexual abuse. The child may be neglected in terms of basic physical care or suffer from being threatened physically or emotionally. Canadian laws require teachers to report incidents of suspected child abuse. Proof is not required — only suspicion based on reasonable grounds. The report must go beyond the school or district administration to social services or the Children's Aid Society.

The abused child demonstrates many of the symptoms described earlier in respect to drug abuse. In addition, physical abuse may be signalled by repeated injuries such as bruises and fractures, cigarette burns, human bite marks, poor hygiene, or torn clothing. General signs of neglect, such as withdrawn behaviour, anger, repressed personality, extreme fear of failure, inhibited speech, negative self-image, inability to play, distrust, aggressiveness and temper tantrums, and inappropriate sexual behaviour are other indicators that abuse may exist. Abused children may overachieve because of a fear of failure. They may have difficulty in trusting adults, and come to school early and leave late. If the student's behaviour or school performance changes abruptly or deteriorates steadily in these areas, the teacher should discuss the problem with the principal and other teachers on staff who know the student. At this level the decision should be made whether to contact social services, police, Children's Aid, or other appropriate agencies.

Teachers' Responses to Child Abuse

How should a teacher respond if a student reports an incident of abuse? Say that it's good that the student told you, that the student is brave, that you believe the student, that the student is not responsible for the abuse, and that you will help the student and things will turn out OK. Do not agree to keep the situation a secret. Tell the student that the incident must be reported in order to stop the abuse. Communicate with school administrators and encourage a team approach with outside agencies.

There have been occasional incidents in which parents, guardians, or teachers have been falsely accused of child abuse. As a result, the positive closeness between teacher and student has been lost to some extent in today's schools, and males in daycare centres and primary grades are automatically viewed with some suspicion. With these important qualifiers in mind, however, teachers still have a responsibility for the protection of students.

Responding to Discipline Problems

Following are several examples of actual discipline problems experienced by beginning teachers. Use the information provided earlier in the chapter to determine procedures a teacher should follow in each situation. What is the key to the problem? Which alternative should be selected? What should the teacher do?

CASE STUDY 11-1: CONTROLLING AND CHANNELLING

STUDENT ENTHUSIASM

The teacher has planned a science demonstration. She has brought new materials and set them on a table. The students are very enthused about these materials at the demonstration table. The teacher has encouraged the students to come to the table and help her set up the materials. Within minutes students are clustering around the teacher, anxious to manipulate various items on the table. Many are out of their seats and manipulating the apparatus on their own before the teacher can demonstrate it.

The teacher demands that some students return to their desks and sit. However, within a few minutes these same students are back at the table because they cannot withhold their excitement to be involved with other students.

Also, the teacher interrupts students before they can finish their thoughts. She often says "You mean . . ." before the student has finished talking. As a result, many students feel unrecognized and frustrated.

What should the teacher do? Consider some of these alternatives and add other possibilities you might think about in this situation.

1. Stop the attempt to set up the materials and require all students to return to their desks. Have them take out books and return to seatwork to get things under control.
2. Harness the interest and enthusiasm by establishing one or two firm rules, such as "Raise your hand when you want everyone's attention."
3. Emphasize positive behaviour. Avoid interrupting students in the middle of what they are trying to say.
4. Move quickly into the demonstration. Avoid losing momentum by trying to gain complete order in the classroom. Move the lesson quickly to a follow-up assignment.
5. The problem in this situation is how to channel student enthusiasm. The teacher has been unable to deflect this enthusiastic behaviour. Confrontation and control is not the best solution. Rather, the enthusiasm needs to be deflected in other ways.

There are times when the energy of students cannot be controlled or stifled. The best course of action then is to move into lessons quickly and maintain a brisk pace. Sometimes lessons fall apart because teachers insist on complete control before proceeding.

CASE STUDY 11-2: A NEW ENVIRONMENT

The teacher has brought the class to the stage behind the gymnasium. She wants to demonstrate geometry principles with strings and large cardboard triangles. Students are asked to stand in a circle on the stage around the teacher. Pylons mark points on the circle.

A basketball game is going on in a Phys Ed class behind the curtain on the gym floor. In addition to the noise factor, some students are horsing around with the basketball players, poking metre sticks through the stage curtain.

The problem is that the teacher has taken students to a new environment — from the classroom to the stage. Students are no longer sitting in desks but are standing or sitting on the floor. They have grouped by choice, resulting in some groups being inattentive. Private conversations begin to occur. Pylons are used for hockey goal posts and the metre sticks as hockey sticks by some students. The students are arranged in a circle with the teacher in the centre, which provides no perceptual awareness of the total group by the teacher.

What are the alternatives for the teacher? The teacher could return the class to the classroom. It is advisable to know when to retreat! Another alternative is to demand that established rules of order be followed. The teacher needs to be strict and assertive in this situation. Rules such as raising hands, sitting on lines drawn on the floor, and selection of group members by the teacher, rather than permitting self-selection of groups, should be enforced. Make groups or teams accountable for specific tasks. Quicken the pace of the lesson.

In summary, the teacher could (a) while still in the classroom, prepare the students for the new environment, (b) establish clear rules and procedures, (c) quicken the pace, and (d) ensure individual and group accountability.

There are other situations in which students are taken to new environments. For example, teachers take their students outside onto the school grounds for physical education or to demonstrate things such as directions and surveys. Students may be taken from the home classroom to a new classroom, to the gymnasium, to the shop, or on field trips. Each of these new environments requires additional attention by teachers in order to avoid classroom management problems.

CASE STUDY 11-3: CONFRONTATION

A student arrives late to class. He missed yesterday's exam, and the teacher wants him to write the exam now. The student replies "I'm not prepared. I won't write it now." A debate follows in front of the class. Other students get involved and side with the student. The teacher gets angry and orders some students out of the room.

What are some potential alternatives for the teacher in this situation?

1. Give the student the choice of writing the exam immediately or accepting a zero.
2. Ask the student to commit himself for a time to write the exam.
3. Give the student the choice of either writing the exam now or receiving a penalized mark.
4. Demand that the student leave the room and report to the principal's office for disciplinary action.
5. Dismiss from the room those students who have become involved in the discussion.
6. Avoid the situation by saying "We will decide about this later."

This situation is a case of the public versus private confrontation. Confronting a student in front of other students can create a ripple effect: the whole class may get involved and side with the student against the teacher. Such situations should be avoided. It is difficult to make fair decisions in the heat of the moment. Time is required for reassessment. A teacher needs to remember that some room must be left for both parties to save face. It is not necessary or desirable to push students into a corner where they have, in effect, no breathing room left. Sometimes teachers must back off to a degree in order to solve discipline problems and maintain students' respect.

CASE STUDY 11-4: THE UNEXPECTED

The topic for the lesson was Christopher Columbus's voyage to the New World. The teacher planned to begin the lesson by asking students to look out the window and tell him what the horizon looked like. He was expecting students to say that it looked flat, and it would be easy to conclude that the earth was flat rather than round. When the question was asked, students quickly chorused "The earth is pear-shaped!"

The teacher did not expect this response. He angrily told the class to stop being smart-alecs. Several students challenged him to go down the hall and talk with the science teacher, who had told them that the earth was actually pear-shaped if the waters of the Pacific and Atlantic oceans were removed. Discussion ensued about whether or not this was an acceptable interpretation of the shape of the earth. The original intent of the question — to lead into the voyage of Christopher Columbus — was lost in the discussion.

What should the teacher have done to avoid a debate over a topic which led away from the intent of his initial question?

1. Use some humour with a comment such as "Perhaps the earth would be good to eat!"
2. Accept the unexpected response and talk about it for a while.
3. Tell the students the answer you were expecting and how it related to Christopher Columbus's voyage.

Be prepared to make changes from your prepared lesson plan. Have some backup procedures or materials available in case part of your lesson does not work out the way you intended it.

CASE STUDY 11-5: MOMENTUM

Students had been outside and came huffing and puffing into the classroom. They were still talking about a variety of things from the previous class, which had been exciting. The teacher wanted to get started with the lesson because there was a great deal to do that day. The teacher said "We will not begin until everyone is listening to me." Most students turned to listen, but several groups continued their conversations. The teacher repeated her remark several times, but the class continued to be noisy. She refused to begin the lesson until there was complete silence and attention. By that time, however, nearly ten minutes of class time had been consumed.

There are some alternatives the teacher could have tried:

1. Raise her voice in anger until everyone is attentive.
2. Flick off the lights.
3. Have a rule such as raising hands for silence.
4. Begin the class immediately. Get most started and the rest will soon fall into line.

CASE STUDY 11-6: SPACE AND TIME

He has just transferred into the school. His hair is long and he wears a black leather jacket and high-top boots. He gives the impression that he is tough and part of an "in" crowd. Some of the girls are fascinated with their new classmate. He also has a hair-trigger temper that flares up frequently. In this particular incident, the class had just ended and the students had started into the hallway. There was the usual chattering and joking among the students. One girl poked the new boy and made fun of him. His temper flared and he ran after her in the crowded hallway. As he neared her, she ducked and he stumbled over the top of her, landing head-first on the floor. He had been embarrassed in front of the other students. As he got to his feet and started to turn around, she tripped him again. He was ready to hit her with a solid punch when the teacher intervened. The boy angrily stormed down the hall. The teacher marched down the hall after him, demanding that he stop. The boy broke into a run and the teacher followed. The boy dashed into the washroom and barricaded himself behind the door. In a moment a crowd of students gathered around the washroom door to see the excitement. Several other students heard the commotion and came out of the library.

The teacher asked one of the students to call the principal. When the principal came he tried to calm everyone down, sending the students back to their rooms. Speaking through the closed door, the principal told the boy he could come out and talk whenever he wanted. No one was going to try to push the door open. He told the student that one of the teachers, who had this student in her class, would be designated to talk to him whenever he was ready.

Did the principal take the right action? Should the door have been pushed open and the student pulled from the washroom? What are the implications of doing or not doing this? Did the teacher take the proper action in the hallway after the boy had stumbled over one of the girls?

The principal recognized the need for a student to have some space and time alone. It is difficult to act rationally or make reasonable decisions in the heat of the moment. Sometimes students need time to sort things out for themselves rather than always having a teacher solve their problems. For this reason, some schools have a "time out" room. There are times in which the best policy is to back off for the moment and give the student some breathing room.

CASE STUDY 11-7: JURISDICTION

The teacher on supervision turned the corner and saw two students struggling, one trying to shove the other into a locker. The teacher had to respond and maintain physical safety immediately. One of the students could easily get bruised or cut on the metal doors of the locker.

The teacher marched up to the struggling students and shouted "Stop this right now." The students were ordered to go into the schoolyard and gather paper until the bell. At the bell they were to report to the principal's office.

The students quickly stopped their pushing and shoving and went out into the schoolyard. The teacher on supervision thought he had handled the situation well, until another teacher approached him angrily and asked "Did you realize I had a major exam scheduled for my students at the beginning of the last period?" A staff conflict had arisen.

Who has jurisdiction over students in public areas of the school such as the gymnasium, hallways, and grounds? How else should the teacher on supervision have handled this situation? This example illustrates the need for staff co-operation in dealing with discipline.

Chapter Twelve:

THE EVALUATION PROCESS

Main Understandings

In this chapter you will learn the following:

1. Evaluation can be used for different purposes.
2. Evaluation should occur in all areas of learning— knowledge, skills, values, attitudes, and appreciations.
3. Evaluation should measure the objectives which were determined at the outset of teaching.
4. Some approaches in collecting evaluation information are more effective than others.
5. How a teacher analyzes information used to evaluate students should be consistent with one's philosophy about evaluation.
6. Evaluation should be reported clearly and honestly.
7. Decisions about students and future teaching strategies should be based on effective evaluation.

Assessment of students is a significant part of teaching. As illustrated in Figure 12.1, a teacher progresses through several stages when evaluating students. After determining the purposes and objectives of

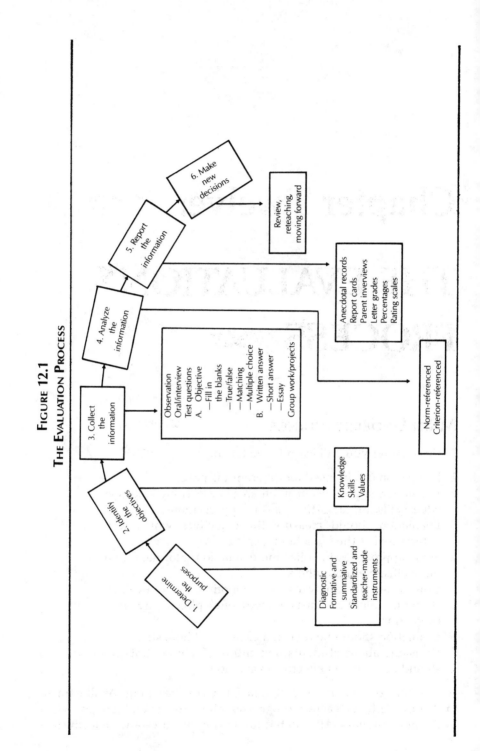

FIGURE 12.1
THE EVALUATION PROCESS

evaluation, information is collected and analyzed. Eventually it must be reported back to students, parents or guardians, and school authorities. This information is used to make decisions with respect to student performance and placement in the school system.

Evaluation must take individual learning differences into account. Gifted students should be challenged to identify relationships between concepts, and to determine or predict changes in these relationships. Memorizing rules and procedures in mathematics, for example, is insufficient. These students should be asked to explain the reasons underlying such rules. Opportunities to exercise creative thought should be a substantial component of the evaluation.

Students with learning disabilities should also be evaluated, but in a way that will minimize the effects of the learning disability. For example, the teacher could use study guides or short-answer questions, or accept oral answers or answers on a word processor. These students could also be given additional time to complete an activity, and the teacher could read aloud instructions and/or test questions to them.

Assessment involves two activities: measurement and evaluation. Measurement, the initial step, is the process of determining a grade which reflects performance. The second step, evaluation, judges the value or worth of that performance. The different purposes for evaluation are seen below:

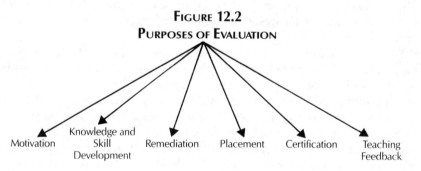

FIGURE 12.2
PURPOSES OF EVALUATION

Motivation | Knowledge and Skill Development | Remediation | Placement | Certification | Teaching Feedback

Effective evaluation requires a teacher to respond to six major questions:

1. *Why* am I evaluating my students?
2. Does my evaluation reflect my *objectives*?
3. Which is the best way to *collect* information that will evaluate my students?
4. How should the information be *analyzed*?
5. How should the information be *reported* to students and parents?
6. Which *decisions* should be made as a result of the evaluation?

DETERMINE THE PURPOSES

Why evaluate students? Evaluation can be done to *motivate* students to learn. Testing to review work is common. Unless students are assigned a test or project that will be graded, some will not read or study. Not everyone is motivated to learn merely for the sake of learning. Students expect to be evaluated on their schoolwork. They want feedback on what they have accomplished in class.

Evaluation can be used to analyze errors and provide a basis for *remedial* work. It can determine skills required to perform subsequent work. *Readiness tests* help determine if students have the prerequisite skills for further work. They are often used in Mathematics and in English/ Language Arts. *Diagnostic evaluation* is used for learning purposes rather than for judgment or grading purposes.

Parents, students, and the school system expect marks periodically throughout the year, and these marks must be based on some acceptable form of evaluation. *Placement tests* help determine which programs are best suited for students, which units of work need to be modified, skipped, or repeated, and whether or not a more advanced level of instruction is best.

Some evaluation is done to establish proficiency by recognizing a student's attainment of a minimum or acceptable level of competence. This evaluation leads to *certification*. Examples include tests for a driver's licence, first-aid certificates, swimming certificates, levels of attainment in music, etc.

Finally, evaluation provides *feedback* on how well something has been taught. If all students fail, perhaps the work was too difficult, students did not study — or the teaching was inadequate!

Depending on the purpose of evaluation, testing may occur before, during, or after instruction. Will the evaluation be used as a pretest, as part of formative evaluation, or for summative evaluation? Pretesting occurs before instruction. It is diagnostic testing. It answers the questions "Are students ready for further work? Do they need remedial work in some areas?"

Formative and Summative Evaluation

Evaluation should be both formative and summative in nature.

Formative evaluation refers to evaluation which occurs throughout the teaching of a topic or unit of study. Assessment in skills development frequently lends itself to evaluation during a unit. Marking student notebooks is part of formative evaluation. In-class assignments, group projects, and periodic tests may be part of formative evaluation as well. The purpose of formative evaluation is to avoid basing the entire grade on a single test or assignment at the end of the unit.

Summative evaluation occurs at the end or summation of a unit of study. Usually this occurs in the form of a unit-end test, although an exam is not the only form of summative evaluation. Summative evaluation may be a final project or other special assignment which is due after the conclusion of a unit of study.

The following example combines formative and summative evaluation.

Unit Evaluation

Assignment	Value	Due Date
Contribution to the Group Project	15%	March 3
Test on Map Work	10%	March 8
Written Report on a Special Topic	20%	March 14
Neat Notebook	20%	March 15
Bulletin Board Display	10%	March 18
Final Test	25%	March 20
	100%	

In this example for evaluating a unit of study, the teacher has identified each part of the evaluation and indicated the relative worth of each. The first four items occurred during the teaching of the unit and therefore constituted formative evaluation. Students were required to cut or sketch pictures on particular themes and organize a bulletin-board display by the end of the unit. This assignment, along with the final test, constituted the summative evaluation of the unit.

Note that this teacher has identified the due dates for the various assignments. This is important to help students plan. Once a due date for an assignment has been established, it is important that the teacher stick to it if at all possible. If an extension is given, those who planned and worked to meet the deadline are, in effect, penalized while those who did not plan or work hard enough are rewarded. Changing due dates without a good reason teaches students to procrastinate.

Standardized and Teacher-Made Tests

The distinction between teacher-made tests and standardized tests is important. The advantage of employing tests devised by the teacher is that objectives specific to a particular class or unit of instruction are evaluated.

Standardized tests are designed by experts unfamiliar with the backgrounds and capabilities of your students. They are administered to large groups of students to determine norms which allow comparisons with a wide segment of students in the same grade or same subject across the country. These types of tests are achievement tests which measure basic skills or general knowledge.

Other types of standardized tests are intelligence tests, aptitude tests, personality tests, tests of basic reading abilities, map interpretation tests, tests for mathematical comprehension, and perceptual awareness tests. Standardized tests provide teachers with a broader perspective within which to evaluate students, whereas teacher-made tests evaluate students on skills and knowledge which have been specifically taught in class. Both types of tests provide information used for evaluating students.

IDENTIFY THE OBJECTIVES

What did you want your students to learn? What did you want them to be able to do? These are fundamental questions to answer when deciding how to evaluate students. After you have reflected upon what you have taught, connect the three basic elements of teaching: objectives, methods/activities, and evaluation.

Be certain that your evaluation relates directly to your original objectives.

Students' knowledge, skills, and values should all be evaluated. Knowledge can be evaluated through written or oral assignments and tests. Skill development can be assessed with the aid of a checklist which identifies certain skills or subcomponents of a skill. Values can be evaluated by giving students a social or moral problem to consider and then asking them to identify the main issue or problem, provide alternate solutions to the problem, and identify consequences of the various alternatives. Attitude scales and inventories may be used as well. Asking students to respond to particular situations in terms of "How might this person feel?" or "How do you feel?" may be used to assess tolerance or empathy.

COLLECT THE INFORMATION

Various techniques are used to collect information with which to evaluate students. These measurement techniques include anecdotal records, checklists based on observations, oral interviews, written tests, and rating scales to measure skills, group work, projects, and performances in public speaking, music, physical education, etc.

Observations and Anecdotal Records

Observation of students can be carried out formally or informally. Informal observation occurs during daily lessons. Are students paying attention? Are they following directions? Are they able to do the work?

Anecdotal records are brief written narratives of specific observations. In past years the writing of anecdotal records was more common. Teachers wrote summary assessments of students at the end of the school term. Although valuable information was made available, some of this information was too general. It was based on limited information and tended to stereotype students or student behaviour.

When creating anecdotal records, teachers need to be careful not to make comments which might be misinterpreted at a later date

---

Observations need to be translated into written form to provide a basis for judgments. For example, a teacher could make check marks on a class seating plan each time a student speaks out of turn, gets into a disagreement with another student, or provides off-topic or wrong responses during a class discussion. In the example below information is used to judge a student's attentiveness in class.

Student: John Reynolds

Off-Task Times

10:05-10:07 — Gazing out the window.
10:12-10:15 — Talking to another student.
10:20-10:22 — Playing with a pencil and doodling on a piece of paper.
10:25-10:35 — Looking at unrelated picture cards.
10:35-10:40 — Gazing out the window.

When observing students for evaluation purposes:

1. Limit the observations to one specific aspect of behaviour.
2. Define the context of the observation in detail.
3. Describe behaviour only. Avoid making inferences, drawing conclusions, or inserting personal opinions.
4. Collect some written information. Conclusions made later should be based on actual (written) evidence.
5. Make several observations.
6. Ask someone else to make a few observations.

The following is an example of an anecdotal record based on the observation of a student. It describes behaviour only. Judgments will be made later.

Terry was observed during four recess periods between January 9 and 12. He used 7 swear words, made 18 negative references about other children, and got into 3 pushing/shoving situations. Nearly all occurred in the last five minutes of the recess period. His conflicts occurred with four boys and one girl. Nineteen of the 28 conflict episodes occurred with one other classmate — Henry.

Observations may occur during science demonstrations, class reports, playing a musical instrument, or working in groups. Teachers gain valuable insights by observing students in different situations — during study periods, at recess, in the library, on the playground, in the gymnasium, after school, at a school dance, during a class party, etc.

Oral Interviews

Oral interviews are a less common but nevertheless potentially valuable technique in acquiring information for evaluating students. The following guidelines help teachers conduct effective interviews:

1. Be clear in your own mind about the specific topics and questions you wish to discuss during the interview.
2. Note the student's feelings about the topic in addition to knowledge of the topic.
3. Ask related questions based on what the student has said during the interview.
4. Listen to what the student is saying. Avoid writing notes or using a tape recorder while interviewing the student, as this can be distracting.
5. Ask for examples to clarify various points.
6. Ask the student to verbally summarize major points and principles.

Tests and Examinations

Principles for constructing good tests. Every test should have content validity. In other words, it should test the important parts of what has been taught. This can be checked by looking at your original objectives and relating the test items to these objectives. For example, if a major objective is to have students learn about the physical geography of the North, a test item which asks students to describe Inuit cultural characteristics would lack content validity. A primary teacher who wants children to learn traffic safety rules would not ask students to name the different kinds of vehicles (cars, bicycles, trucks, etc.) that are on the street. Focus on one major objective when determining what to test.

Items on a test should be common. When students respond to different test items, it is difficult to determine a common basis for assessment. This occurs when students are given choices of questions to answer, unless these questions are designed precisely to measure the same skills or content.

All students should have the same amount of time to write the test, and it should be sufficient so everyone has ample time to complete it. This enables everyone to perform to the limits of their abilities.

Directions should be clear and concise. Allow students to ask questions for clarification. Tests for older students should indicate the relative value of each question, and the criteria for marking. ·

Other practices in test situations are important. Students should be told why they are taking the test. Is it for learning, identifying weaknesses, review, or a final grade? Tests should be given only after ample time for review and study has been provided. Students should know beforehand what will be emphasized on the test. Surprise tests are pedagogically unacceptable and students consider them unfair. They catch students off-guard and do little to prepare them for success.

Content-specific and skill-testing questions. Test questions can be categorized into two types: content-specific and skill-testing.

Content-specific questions are answered from memory. No information is given to students. After learning a subject, students must remember what they learned in order to answer the questions. For example, after learning about electricity, students could be asked specific questions such as: "Identify at least three major sources of electricity." "Calculate the kilowatt hours used if a one-horsepower motor runs for seven hours." "What is the purpose of a circuit-breaker?" The questions might be in various forms — short answer, multiple choice, calculation, or matching. Regardless of the type of question, the common characteristic is that students must draw on specific information and skills learned in previous classes.

Skill-testing questions provide students with information and ask students to interpret it. Both knowledge and skills learned must be used to answer the questions. Again, the form of the question can vary — short answer, multiple choice, etc.

Information given students in the test question could be in the form of a chart, graph, diagram, map, tape recording, cartoon, or written passage. After teaching a unit on the media, a teacher might require students to use both knowledge about media and the skill of summarizing information to answer the following test question:

Everyone watches television. Some research indicates that children's aggressive behaviour increases after watching violence on TV. They watch murders, rapes, beatings, stabbings, shootings, and violence in living colour. Scheming, cheating, and lying are part of many TV shows. On the other hand, there are many educational shows ranging from programs like "Sesame Street" to tips on fishing, travel, and exercise. Television programs on life in other countries and news programs broaden children's horizons. Entertainment is another spinoff from watching TV. It provides relaxation through game shows, comedies, and sports.

Which statement best summarizes this passage?

A. There is too much violence on TV.
B. Humour and entertainment are important spinoffs from TV.
C. Sports and entertainment are good things about TV.
D. Children are influenced by TV.
E. A person should not watch too much TV.

In the example, students are required to extrapolate the main message or summary of the article. These types of questions can be designed so students must:

1. Search for specific information (e.g., by interpreting a graph or performing mathematical calculations).
2. Summarize information (e.g., "What is the author's intent?").
3. Draw inferences (e.g., What are the implications? If this is a cause, what might the effects be? What does it mean?).

Another way to evaluate students is through "select" and 'supply" questions. "Select" questions require students to select an answer from information given in the test item. Examples include True/False, matching, and multiple-choice questions. "Supply" questions are those which require students to supply an answer. These include short-answer and essay questions.

Questions which require students to select the correct answer can be quickly and objectively marked. They can cover a wide range of information. The disadvantage of these types of questions is that they require only the recall of specific detail rather than the application of higher levels of thinking. Students who are poor readers can be at a disadvantage trying to respond to these questions.

The advantage of supply-type questions is that they enable students to be creative and require higher levels of thinking. Students have the opportunity to tell or display all that they know relevant to the question. However, such responses are more difficult to mark objectively. They also place students who are weak in writing skills at a disadvantage. Since there are advantages and disadvantages to both types of questions, a good testing program would provide students with opportunities to respond to both types of questions.

Fill-in-the-blank questions. Also referred to as completion questions, fill-in-the-blank questions can be quickly constructed and easily marked. The disadvantages of these questions are that they emphasize memory, and ambiguous wording of the question could mean that more than one answer would be correct. Their value in assessing deeper understanding is limited. The following are some guidelines for constructing fill-in-the-blank questions.

1. Place the blank near the end of the statement. This enables students to understand the content of the question without having to go back to the beginning of the statement to provide the answer. For example, "Lizards and snakes are classified as reptiles" is better than "Reptiles include lizards and snakes."
2. Write the statement so that only one answer is correct. For example, "The *longest* river in Canada is called the Mackenzie" is preferable to "The *biggest* river in Canada is called the ____."
3. Avoid more than one blank in the statement. Multiple blanks are confusing and difficult to answer. For example, "Moisture that falls in the summer is called rain" is better than "Moisture that falls from the sky is called rain, sleet, snow, and hail."
4. The word to be filled in should be an important word in the statement. For example, "The process of creating an electric current by moving a wire loop through a magnetic field is called induction." This statement would be less useful if the word "loop" was left blank. "Induction" is the significant concept in this test item.
5. To increase the quality of fill-in-the-blank questions, a teacher can write "comparison" or "logic" questions, in which students are required to find the connection between two pieces of information. For example, "Snakes are to reptiles as horses are to mammals." "Winter is to snow as summer is to rain."

True/false questions. True/false questions can be quickly scored. A major disadvantage is that students who know nothing about the topic have a 50-50 chance of guessing the correct answer. To discourage guessing, use rules for scoring such as "right minus wrong" or "right minus one-half the number wrong." Such rules usually are perceived negatively by students. As with fill-in-the-blank questions, true/false items should be used sparingly by teachers wanting to develop high-quality evaluations. Here are some guidelines for constructing true/false questions:

1. Write short and simple statements. For example:

   T F Spruce trees grow in Canada.

   An unnecessarily long and confusing statement would be:

   T F Spruce trees grow throughout many regions of Canada but not in many parts of the country.

2. Statements should be unquestionably true or false.

   T F Robin Hood lived in England.

T　F　King Arthur was the leader of the Knights of the Round Table.

A poor-quality item would be only partially true or false:

T　F　Both Robin Hood and King Arthur lived in England and Robin Hood was the leader of the Knights of the Round Table.

3. Avoid using words which give clues that the statement is true or false.

T　F　An increase in horsepower always results in greater power.

A better statement would be:

T　F　An increase in horsepower usually results in greater power.

4. Design statements which enable students to correct the incorrect statements. This greatly increases the quality of the items.

T　F　If the sides of a triangle have lengths a, b, and c, and $a^2 + b^2 = c^2$, then the triangle is (an) a equilateral triangle (right angle).

Matching questions. Matching questions are quickly and objectively scored to measure factual information. (Better readers hold a distinct advantage in completing matching questions correctly.) For example:

Match Countries and Capital Cities

Directions: Write the letter of the item in Column B that best fits the item in Column A. Write your answer in the blank on the left. Items in Column B may be used once only.

	Column A	*Column B*
(J) ____	Canada	A. Berlin
(F) ____	Japan	B. Beijing
(H) ____	United States	C. Hong Kong
(D) ____	France	D. Paris
(A) ____	Germany	E. Moscow
		F. Tokyo
		G. New York
		H. Washington, D.C.
		I. London
		J. Ottawa

Here are some guidelines for constructing effective matching questions:

1. Write items with common characteristics in each column.
2. If statements are to be used, place the written statements in Column A. Students can more easily read the statement first and then search Column B for the correct response.

3. There should be a larger number of items in Column B than in Column A. Unequal numbers makes guessing more difficult.
4. Avoid long lists. These can become confusing and difficult to read.
5. All responses should be plausible.
6. Avoid drawing lines to connect the two columns. This can be confusing to both student and marker. (In early primary grades this technique may be appropriate for brief matching questions.)
7. Place all of the items in the question on the same page. Students should not have to flip pages to complete the question.
8. State whether items in Column B may be used once only or more than once.

Multiple-choice questions. Multiple-choice items are difficult to write but easy to mark and can provide students with greater challenges than fill-in-the-blank, true/false, or matching questions. The choices must be carefully worded, or some students will find clues which enable them to guess at the answers. Students should be advised to begin by eliminating the most unlikely alternatives, thus increasing their chances of selecting the correct responses. Here are some guidelines for constructing good multiple-choice questions:

1. The stem should be longer than the choices. For example:

   What is the name of an act which treats people on the basis of unfair criteria?
   A. sexism
   B. hatred
   C. prejudice
   D. discrimination
   E. racism

   When the choices are longer than a brief stem, the question becomes very difficult to read and may no longer measure what students actually know.
2. All alternatives should have some merit, but there should be only one correct or "best" answer. Avoid choices which are obviously incorrect.
3. The question should be phrased as a complete sentence. Incomplete statements create reading difficulties for students.
4. Keep the length of the choices consistent.
5. Avoid wording the questions negatively. Negative wording tends to confuse students and thus fails to measure what they know.
6. Avoid giving clues. Key words in the stem should not be used in one of the choices.
7. Arrange the choices randomly.
8. Avoid too much use of "a and b above," "all of the above," and "none of the above."

Refer to the above guidelines to determine why the following examples are *not* good multiple-choice items.

1. Discrimination is:

   A. a criminal act which involves negative behaviour toward a group of people.

   B. an act which creates a sense of terror in the minds of innocent people.

   C. any thought or act which is directed against a visible minority within a country.

   D. any thought which thinks of another group of people as inferior to oneself.

   E. any act which treats people on the basis of unfair criteria.

2. In the play "Colours," which theme applies to Act II?

   A. Honesty.

   B. Attraction.

   C. Bravery in the sense that one should do what he/she knows is right.

   D. Fear.

   E. Respect.

3. Which lines on a map measure distance north and south of the equator?

   A. Latitude.

   B. Meridian.

   C. Longitude.

   D. a and b above.

   E. All of the above.

4. The product of 50.25 and 101.4 is

   A. 4,998.25

   B. 5,090.64

   C. 5,095.35

   D. 21.19

5. The agreement signed by the Indians and the government was known as a:

   A. Agreement.

   B. Accord.

   C. Arrangement.

   D. Treaty.

   E. Understanding.

6. Which is not a reptile?

   A. Snake.

   B. Lizard.

   C. Bat.

   D. Turtle.

   E. Crocodile.

The guidelines for effective multiple-choice questions which were not followed are indicated below.

Item	Guideline Not Followed
1	1
2	4
3	8
4	2
5	3, 6
6	5

Short-answer questions. Short-answer questions require students to write several sentences. They are easy to construct, but marking them is more subjective. Written answers may be partially correct, so more time and effort is needed to mark them. Poor writers are at a disadvantage. Guessing is unlikely. Here are some guidelines for writing good short-answer questions:

1. Write the directions clearly and concisely so that only a single (and brief) answer can be given. Use specific terms and brief statements. Begin with a question.
2. Prepare a marking guide. Identify the exact criteria for allocating marks. For example:

   What are the major advantages and disadvantages of nuclear power compared to power generated from a fossil-fuel base? Tell why one power source would be preferable to the other.

Criteria: Nuclear power	Marks
- advantages	2
- disadvantages	2
Fossil-fuel-based power	
- advantages	2
- disadvantages	2
Reasons for preferring one source	2
Total marks for the question	10

3. The example above includes a factor which can make short-answer questions better: Have students select a choice and defend it, or argue for or against a selected position.

Essay questions. Essay questions can be designed quickly but are subjective and time-consuming to mark. They allow students to develop their own ideas, tell what they know, and incorporate higher levels of thinking. Good writers have an advantage. Here are some guidelines for constructing good essay questions:

1. Phrase the question in specific terms. Directions such as "Write about nuclear energy" or "What do you think about nuclear energy?" are

too vague. Better directions would be: "Write an essay, four pages in length, about nuclear energy. Give a brief history of its development in your opening paragraph. Most of the essay should be about (a) its scientific principles of operation and (b) its impact on our world today. End your essay with a personal statement of your position on whether or not nuclear energy should be further developed and used."

2. Keep the purpose for writing clearly in mind and communicate it to the students.

3. Follow the practice of "positive marking." First give credit for what the student has done right, and only then deduct marks for errors.

4. Allocate marks according to predetermined criteria. Communicate the criteria to students in advance.

5. Try "aspect marking." First read the paper for an overall impression and assign a letter grade. Each paper is then reread for specific criteria. For example: content, 50 marks; organization, 20 marks; expression, 20 marks; and mechanical accuracy, 10 marks; for a total of 100 marks. In the mechanical accuracy category, one-half mark could be deducted for each error in punctuation or grammar, to a maximum of 20 errors. Some teachers prefer not to penalize the student for identical errors which appear in the same essay.

6. Strive to be neutral and fair in marking. Cover the student's name. Avoid being swayed by personal bias, whatever your reaction may be to opinions and attitudes expressed by the writer. Mark on the basis of the logic of argument and presentation of information. Indicate good points by a check mark in the margin.

Use the guidelines above to decide the best way to handle the following situations which may arise in marking essays.

1. A student totally misinterpreted the question. He was asked to write on "capital punishment" but wrote on "corporal punishment." Using aspect marking, the student could lose only 20 out of 40 marks for content.

2. A student wrote an essay that was far too short. He felt that the less he wrote, the fewer writing errors he would be likely to make.

3. A student wrote a choppy, monotonous paper with short but correct sentences to avoid losing marks on mechanical accuracy.

4. A student wrote a reasonably good essay but lost maximum marks for mechanical accuracy because he is dyslexic.

5. A student wrote an essay taking a position which was totally unacceptable to the views of the examiner (for example, that all politicians are thieves, when the teacher is a former politician).

Problem-solving questions. Problem-solving questions require students to recall and analyze information supplied by the teacher in class to provide a solution (or solutions) to the test question. For example, questions based on the diagram in Figure 12.3 could include "Where does the water flow when the backwash valve is open?" or "What is the purpose of the check valve?" True/false statements can be devised, such as "More water enters the pipe system from the main drain than from the skimmer" (false) or "The backwash valve prevents water from being pumped into the ground or into a drain" (true). Multiple-choice statements such as the following could be designed:

Where in the diagram does water enter the plumbing system?
   A. Near the bottom.
   B. Near the top.
   C. On the left-hand side.
   D. On the right-hand side.
   E. From all four sides.

FIGURE 12.3

SWIMMING-POOL PLUMBING

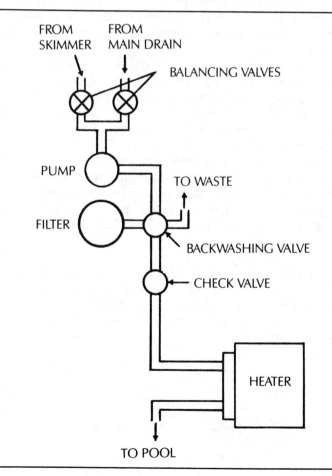

A question requiring students to write answers about the piping system could be devised. Regardless of the type of test questions, a test item which requires students to analyze information given them can be a high-quality test item.

ANALYZE THE MARKS

Once marks have been acquired for students (through tests, assignments, projects, etc.), how should these marks be graded or evaluated? Two approaches to grading might be considered: criterion-referenced and norm-referenced.

In criterion-referenced grading, the students must either meet the criterion or receive a failing grade. For example, a teacher might say that 50 percent is the pass mark on the test. Anyone not receiving 50 percent or higher fails. It doesn't matter what the class's pattern of results is; the criterion was set beforehand.

Norm-referenced grading occurs when student marks are placed on the normal curve. This approach assumes that in any group there will be a few who will do very well on the test, a few who can be grouped at the bottom of the range of test scores, and the majority who will fall in the middle of the range. If a test is very difficult, a top score of 45 percent might be considered an excellent mark, and an A grade might be given to that student. On the other hand, on a very easy test the lowest mark might be 70 percent, and it would be considered a failure grade because everyone else in the group received 75 percent or higher.

The form of grading is determined by the school or school district. Three approaches are common. Summarizing statements occur in the lower grades: "Sarah is achieving beyond expectations in math." "Lenny does not know his basic number facts yet." Letter grades — A, B, C, D, E, F — are used at times. Percentile grades are also used in the upper years.

Grades can be converted from raw scores to percent and/or letter grades. In the following example, class scores on a test are ranked and converted to percent or letter grades. Where groups of scores can be identified, students in the various groups can be assigned a letter grade. The percent column is based on criterion-referenced grading; the letter grades on norm-referenced grading.

Converting Student Marks

Raw Scores	Percent	Student Names	Letter Grade
25	100%		A
24	96%	Sarah, John, Raji	
23	92%	Mike, Tammy	
22	88%		

21	84%		B
20	80%	Tera, Najah, Bill	
19	76%	Susan, Jodi	
18	72%		
17	68%		C
16	64%	Odi, Petra, Li	
15	60%	Yeswanth	
14	56%		D
13	52%	Jerome, Mary	
12	48%		

REPORT THE GRADES

Anecdotal records may be used to report evaluation to students and parents or guardians. Performance in school may be reported in terms of percent scores or letter grades. Other ways of reporting are checklists, rating scales, and word descriptors.

Checklists

The following is an example of a checklist:

Social Skills

Situations
- Speaks clearly
- Waits for his/her turn
- Offers ideas
- Makes relevant comments
- Does not repeat comments
- Challenges ideas
- Gives reasons for challenging ideas
- Accepts ideas of others

Study Habits
- Does work independent of others
- Goes to work promptly
- Follows directions
  a) Oral
  b) Written
- Arrives in class on time
- Brings necessary supplies to class

Rating Scales

In a rating scale on group work, for example, the teacher would rate each item on a scale such as the following:

Always   Never

Items
1. Does a fair share of the work
2. Contributes ideas

3. Stays on topic
4. Abides by final group decisions
5. Volunteers ideas

Word Descriptors

Word descriptors may be used to report characteristics of students. These words describe the emotional characteristics of a student. These characteristics might be underlined, circled, or checked from a list such as the following:

Cheerful	Troubled	Nervous
Optimistic	Antagonistic	Shy
Pleasant	Boisterous	Sensitive
Confident	Moody	Resentful
Sympathetic	Dreamy	Envious
Generous	Mischievous	Even-tempered
Forgiving	Placid	Hot-tempered

Phrase Descriptors

Social characteristics of students might be assessed with the aid of the items in these columns:

Makes advances to others	Responds to advances by others
Makes friends easily	Finds it difficult to make friends
Socially minded	Individualistic
Has many friends	Has few friends
Liked by the class	Disliked by the class
Popular in class	Avoided by the class
Class leader	Ridiculed by the class
Friendly with everyone	Friends with a small group
Interested in many things	Has few interests

MAKE NEW DECISIONS

What decisions need to be made as a result of the evaluation? Some discussion occurs even before the marks are reported to students or their parents or guardians.

Consider these situations. Which is best? Which is more fair?

1. Should students be given surprise tests? They may keep students alert, but resentment may also result. Using tests just to keep students on their toes is not far from using tests as a form of punishment.

2. Should students be shown how to study for different kinds of tests? Yes. Learning how to write tests is an important educational skill. Test-taking skills are discussed below.
3. When should tests be scheduled? Students are usually sharper in the mornings. Avoid giving tests immediately after a holiday or on the same date another assignment is due. Monday morning tests often are not appreciated by students or parents who have other plans and activities on the weekend.
4. Should tests or assignments be marked harder or easier at different times? One ancient piece of advice has been to mark harder early in the school term. Then it is easier to give higher marks in successive report card periods. Marking harder as the term progresses gives the impression that students are doing poorly. In contrast, marking harder in the beginning enables students to feel more positive about learning when their grades improve in subsequent report periods. Does this seem fair?

   On the other hand, high marks in the beginning are encouraging, and often students will work harder throughout the year to maintain these marks. Is this a better approach? Perhaps it is best to pay little attention to this aspect of grading and try to mark in a consistent manner from the beginning to the end of the whole year.
5. Should students be permitted to rewrite a test if they have done poorly on it? It may be argued that students should have opportunities to improve their marks and correct their errors, and therefore opportunities to rewrite a test should be allowed. However, students who did well may find this unfair, particularly if they studied for the test while the others did not. It may be fair to give one student the opportunity to raise his or her mark only if everyone has the same opportunity. Should the two marks be averaged if students are given the opportunity to rewrite a test, or should only the higher mark be recorded? Communicating the guidelines and expectations to students is very important.

Test-Taking Skills

Sometimes teachers have students write tests and do projects to develop skills. One aspect of writing tests is learning how to take them. Students should be given the following advice: Read all directions first. Do certain questions initially. Eliminate some questions or potential solutions that are less desirable. Judge the time spent on sections of the test in relation to the marks allotted to various parts. Re-read your answers. Avoid changing your mind on answers you have given. Allow time to review. Adjust to pressures involved in evaluation. Skill in taking tests is acquired only through practice.

References

Anderson, L.W. 1989. *The Effective Teacher: Study Guide and Readings*. New York: Random House.

Arends, L.R. 1991. *Learning to Teach*, 2nd ed. New York: McGraw-Hill.

Ausubel, D.P. 1960. "The Use of Advance Organizers in the Learning and Retention of Meaningful Verbal Material," *Journal of Educational Psychology* 51: 267-72.

Behnke, G., and E.N. Labovitz. 1982. "Coping With Classroom Distractions." In *Focus on Teaching: Readings from the Elementary School Journal*, edited by W. Doyle and T. Good. Chicago: University of Chicago Press.

Bloom, B.S., G.F. Madaus, and J.T. Hastings. 1981. *Evaluation to Improve Learning*. New York: McGraw-Hill.

Borich, Gary D. 1988. *Effective Teaching Methods*. Toronto: Merrill.

Brophy, J., and C. Evertson. 1978. "Context Variables in Teaching." *Educational Psychologist* 12: 310-16.

Brophy, J.M., and T.L. Good. 1986. "Teacher Behaviours and Student Achievement." In *Handbook of Research on Teaching*, 3rd ed., edited by M.C. Wittrock. New York: Macmillan.

Callahan, J.F., and L.H. Clark. 1988. *Teaching in the Middle and Secondary Schools*, 3rd ed. New York: Macmillan.

Carson, J.C., and P. Carson. 1984. *Any Teacher Can! Practical Strategies for Effective Classroom Management*. Illinois: Charles C. Tomas.

Charles, C.M. 1985. *Building Classroom Discipline: From Models to Practice*. New York: Longman.

Chiarelott, L., L. Davidman, and K. Ryan. 1990. *Leases on Teaching*. Toronto: Holt, Rinehart and Winston.

Cooper, J.M., ed. 1990. *Classroom Teaching Skills*, 4th ed. Boston: D.C. Heath.

Curwin, L.R., and N.A. Mendler. 1988. *Discipline With Dignity*. Alexandria, VA: Association for Supervision and Curriculum Development.

Doyle, W. 1985. "Recent Research on Classroom Management: Implications for Teacher Preparation." *Teacher Education* 36: 31-35.

Eggen, P., and D. Kauchak. 1988. *Strategies for Teachers*, 2nd ed. Englewood Cliffs, NJ: Prentice-Hall.

Emmer, E.T., C.M. Evertson, and L.M. Anderson. 1982. "Effective Classroom Management at the Beginning of the School Year." In *Focus on Teaching: Readings from the Elementary School Journal*, edited by W. Doyle and T. Good. Chicago: University of Chicago Press.

Evertson, C.M., and E.T. Emmer. 1982. "Preventive Classroom Management." In *Helping Teachers Manage Classrooms*, edited by D.L. Duke. Alexandria, VA: Association for Supervision and Curriculum Development.

Evertson, C.M., E.T. Emmer, B.S. Clements, J.P. Sanford and M.E. Worsham. 1984. *Classroom Management for Elementary Teachers*. Englewood Cliffs, NJ: Prentice-Hall.

Flanders, N. 1970. *Analyzing Teacher Behavior*. Reading, MA: Addison-Wesley.

Fuller, F.F., and O.H. Brown. 1975. "Becoming a Teacher." In *Teacher Education: The 74th Yearbook for the National Society for the Study of Education* (Part II), edited by K. Ryan. Chicago: University of Chicago Press.

Ghosh, R., and D. Ray. 1991. *Social Change and Education in Canada*, 2nd ed. Toronto: Harcourt Brace Jovanovich.

Good, T.H., and J.E. Brophy. 1987. *Looking in Classrooms*, 4th ed. New York: Harper & Row.

Good, T., and D. Grouws. 1981. *Experimental Research in Secondary Mathematics* (Final Report, National Institute of Education Grant No. NIE-G-79-0103). Columbia, MO: University of Missouri, Center for the Study of Social Behavior.

Good, T., D. Grouws, and M. Ebmeier. 1983. *Active Mathematics Teaching*. New York: Longman.

Gump, P.V. 1974. "School Settings and Their Keeping." In *Helping Teachers Manage Classrooms*, edited by D.L. Duke. Alexandria, VA: Association for Supervision and Curriculum Development.

Hargreaves, D.H., S.K. Hestor, and F.J. Miller. 1984. "Rules in Play." In *Classrooms and Staffrooms: The Sociology of Teachers and Teaching*, edited by A. Hargreaves and P. Woods. Milton Keynes, England: Open University Press.

Havighurst, R.J., and P.H. Dreyer. 1975. "Youth and Cultural Pluralism." In *Youth: The 74th yearbook of the National Society for the Study of Education*, edited by R.J. Havighurst and P.H. Dreyer. Chicago: University of Chicago Press.

Hollingsworth, P., and K. Hoover. 1991. *Elementary Teaching Methods*, 4th ed. Toronto: Allyn and Bacon.

Jacobsen, D., P. Eggen, and D. Kauchak. 1989. *Methods for Teaching: A Skills Approach*, 3rd ed. Toronto: Merrill.

Jarolimek, J., and Clifford Foster, Sr. 1989. *Teaching and Learning in the Elementary School*, 4th ed. New York: Macmillan.

Jones, V.F., and L.S. Jones. 1986. *Comprehensive Classroom Management: Creating Positive Learning Environments*, 2nd ed. Boston: Allyn and Bacon.

Joyce, B., and M. Weil. 1986. *Models of Teaching*. Englewood Cliffs, NJ: Prentice-Hall.

Kauchak, D., and P.D. Eggen. 1989. *Learning and Teaching: Research Based Methods*. Toronto: Allyn and Bacon.

Kounin, J.S. 1970. *Discipline and Group Management in Classrooms*. New York: Holt, Rinehart and Winston.

Levine, J. 1989. *Secondary Instruction: A Manual for Classroom Teaching*. Toronto: Allyn and Bacon.

Madike, F. 1980. "Teacher Classroom Behaviors Involved in Microteaching and Student Achievement: A Regression Study." *Journal of Educational Psychology* 72: 265-74.

Maslow, A. 1968. *Toward a Psychology of Being*. New York: Van Nostrand Reinhold.

McDonald, F. 1976. "Report on Phase II of the Beginning Teacher Evaluation Study." *Journal of Teacher Education* 27, no. 1: 39-42.

Moore, D.K. 1989. *Classroom Teaching Skills: A Primer*. Toronto: Random House.

Myers, C., and L. Myers. 1990. *An Introduction to Teaching and Schools*. Toronto: Holt, Rinehart and Winston.

Orlich, D., R. Harder, R. Callahan, D. Kauchak, R. Pendergrass, and A. Keogh. 1990. *Teaching Strategies: A Guide to Better Instruction*, 3rd ed. Toronto: D.C. Heath.

Posner, G.J. 1989. *Field Experience: Methods of Reflective Teaching*. White Plains, NY: Longman.

Quina, J. 1989. *Effective Teaching: Going Beyond the Bell Curve*. New York: Harper & Row.

Rogan, Joseph. 1991. "Testing Accommodations for Students With Disabilities." *The Teaching Professor* (March): 3-4.

Rokeach, M. 1960. *The Open and Closed Mind: Investigations into the Nature of Belief Systems and Personality Systems*. New York: Basic Books.

Rosenshine, B. 1983. Teaching Functions in Instructional Programs. *Elementary School Journal* 83: 335-51.

Rosenshine, B., and R. Stevens. 1986. "Teaching Functions." In *Handbook of Research in Teaching*, edited by M.C. Wittrock. New York: Macmillan.

Sanford, J.P., and C.M. Evertson. 1981. "Classroom Management in a Low S.E.S. Junior High: Three Case Studies." *Teacher Education* 32(1): 5-9.

Stallings, J., M. Needles, and N. Stayrook. 1979. *The Teaching of Basic Reading Skills in Secondary Schools, Phase II and Phase III.* Menlo Park, CA: SRI International.

Wright, C., and G. Nuthall. 1970. Relationships Between Teacher Behaviors and Pupil Achievement in Three Experimental Elementary Science Lessons. *American Educational Research Journal* 7: 477-91.

ADDITIONAL REFERENCES

P. 20 Learning Styles, From A. Gregoric (1985) GREGORIC STYLE DELINEATOR, Maynard Mass.: Gabriel Systems.

P. 23 Split-brain Theory, From B. McCarthy, (1986). THE HEMISPHERIC MODE INDICATOR. Barrington, III: Excel Inc.

P. 57 Behavioural Objectives: From R. Mager, (1962). PREPARING INSTRUCTIONAL OBJECTIVES, Belmont, CA: Fearon.

P. 89 Checklist: Reprinted from PREPARATON FOR CLASSROOM TEACHING EXPERIENCE (Manuscript pilot) by D. Barnett and D. Smith, (1990), Saskatoon: College of Education, University of Saskatchewan.

P. 98–100 Concept: Adapted from J. Bruner, J. Goodnow and G.A. Austin (1967) A STUDY OF THINKING, New York: Science Editions, Inc.

P. 116 Discrepant Information: From J. R. Suchman (1962), THE ELEMENTARY SCHOOL TRAINING PROGRAM IN SCIENTIFIC INQUIRY, Report to the U.S. Office of Education, Project Title VII. Urbane: University of Illinois.

P. 142 Wait Time: From M.B. Rowe (1978), Wait, wait, wait, SCHOOL, SCIENCE AND MATHEMATICS 78, 207–216.

P. 157 Logical Consequences: From R. Dreikurs, and P. Cassel, (1972) DISCIPLINE WITHOUT TEARS, New York: Hawthorn Books.

P. 159 Classroom Meetings: From W. Glasser (1969), SCHOOLS WITHOUT FAILURE, New York: Harper and Row.

P. 166–167 Communication Statements: From A MONOGRAPH ON INTERPERSONAL COMMUNICATIONS, by R. Gemmet, (1977) San Mateo County Superintendent of Schools, Redwood City California (ERIC Document Reproduction Service No. ED 153 323).

P. 168 ADHD: From S. Goldstein and M. Goldstein (1990), MANAGING ATTENTION DISORDERS IN CHILDREN, Toronto: John Wiley and Sons.

P. 186–196 Tests and Examinations: Adapted from N. Gronlund (1988), HOW TO CONSTRUCT ACHIEVEMENT TESTS, Fourth Edition, Englewood Cliffs, N.J.: Prentice Hall.

Index